Glory Days

ALSO BY BILL REYNOLDS

Fall River Dreams

ST. MARTIN'S GRIFFIN

NEW YORK

Glory

Days

A BASKETBALL MEMOIR

BILL REYNOLDS

Design by Kate H. Kim

Library of Congress Cataloging-in-Publication Data

Reynolds, Bill
    Glory days : a basketball memoir / Bill Reynolds.
        p. cm.
    ISBN 0-312-18105-1 (hc)
    ISBN 0-312-20966-5 (pbk)
    1. Reynolds, Bill, 1945- .   2. Basketball players—United
States—Biography.   3. Sportwriters—United States—Biography.
I. Title.
GV884.R49R49   1998
796.323'092—dc21
[B]
                                                              97-40489
                                                              CIP

First St. Martin's Griffin Edition: August 1999

10 9 8 7 6 5 4 3 2 1

Glory
Days

Prologue

I remember exactly when I first realized that basketball was no longer the simple game I had played as a kid.

It was February of 1968. I was playing basketball at Brown and we had just been annihilated by Princeton, then one of the country's top college teams. The five-hour bus ride back to Providence, Rhode Island, was as bleak as winter. While the bus crept along through the dreary Jersey meadows, I sat in a window seat feigning sleep. All around me in the darkened bus were teammates slumped in their seats, some sleeping, some just sitting there quietly. The air smelled of failure. If we had had any illusions about ourselves as a team, a 58-point drubbing had shattered them.

As it had shattered any illusions about myself as an athlete. The game had been a defining moment, when I first came face-to-face with my own athletic mortality, the painful realization that I wasn't as good as I hoped, and I never would be.

What was I going to do with this realization? I didn't have a clue.

For I had been brought up to believe in that most American of beliefs: if you worked hard enough, desired something enough, sacrificed enough, your dreams could come true. I had heard it at basketball camps from a succession of speakers. I had read it in the biographies of great athletes. I had absorbed it from coaches. Do more windsprints. Practice more jumpers. Work harder. That belief had been taped on the walls of every locker room. When the going gets tough, the tough get going. . . . It's not the size of the dog in the fight, but the size of the fight in the dog. . . . Winners never quit, and quitters never win. . . . Inspirational clichés, the mantras of my childhood. Simplistic slogans that had begun seducing me at an early age, slogans deeply imbedded in the culture, slogans essentially unquestioned, unchallenged.

Until that night, I had clung to the naive belief I could somehow be a professional basketball player, if not in the NBA, then in the new upstart ABA, a league full of players that no one had ever heard about in college. Hadn't I gotten better every year? Hadn't I been one of the leading scorers in the Ivy League the year before? Hadn't my picture been in several national basketball magazines? Wasn't I due to end my career as one of the top ten scorers in Brown University history? Hadn't I somehow managed to be successful throughout my career, even as the competition had gotten better?

That night, though, I had played against a Princeton sophomore named Geoff Petrie, about whom I had known little. Back then freshmen were ineligible for the varsity, so I hadn't played against Petrie the year before, had only read about him in basketball magazines. Three years later Petrie would be the co-rookie of the year in the NBA, yet I didn't have to be a visionary to know that he already was bigger, stronger, quicker than I was, such a better player that I knew it was folly to consider myself as anything more than what I was: a decent college player on a mediocre-at-best team. That was what all the practice and all the hours and all the bus rides had made me: a decent player, nothing more. A decent player in a college world full of them. A player whose career was going to end in a month.

So I sat by the window running the past through my mind as if it were a newsreel, my despair increasing with each passing mile. Eventually, as if crossing some emotional line, the despair turned to disgust. And I thought about how sick I was of basketball. Sick of playing. Sick of practicing. Sick of even thinking about it.

Which might have been the most unsettling realization of all. For basketball always had been more than just a game to me. It had been a way of life. It had determined who my friends were, where I went to school, what I studied once I got there. For nearly a decade there hadn't been a day when I didn't think about it. Without it, I certainly wouldn't have been at Brown, probably wouldn't have been at any school. Without basketball my life undoubtedly would have been very different. Now I suddenly wondered what it had all been for.

I was a college senior, two courses short of graduating with my class that spring, without any idea of what I wanted to do in the future. It was 1968, three-quarters through the most turbulent decade in American history, when it often seemed as if the nation was undergoing a nervous breakdown. It also was a time of dizzying social change, of the civil rights movement, the antiwar movement, the rise of the counterculture: tremors through a society, shock waves that would change it

forever. Here it was going on all around me, yet I knew little
of it.

Why?

Why didn't I know anything about theater? About art?
About literature? Why had I only read a handful of books in
the past decade? Why was my life so one-dimensional? Why
was my life both defined and shaped by a childhood obsession
with a game? My past was a mélange of empty gyms, taped
ankles, pregame pep talks, echoes of muted cheers. My life revolved around whether my jump shot went in or not.

Was there life after basketball?

I didn't know. Nor did I know then that this childhood obsession with basketball would forever shape my life in ways I
couldn't possibly comprehend at the time. I also didn't understand then that my obsession, what I saw as little more
than my own personal story, was much more universal than I
ever could have envisioned; was, in fact, one of the great unwritten stories, one of the reasons that we as a society are not
only obsessed with sports, but treat great athletes as if they are
somehow descended from kings.

Was there life after basketball?

At twenty-two, on a cold night in the winter of 1968, sitting on that bus watching the future unfold ahead of me like
headlights illuminating the darkened highway, I wasn't sure.

Sports were the glue that held my family together.
Eventually they wouldn't be strong enough to continue to bind us, but I didn't know that back in the tail end of the sleepy Eisenhower 1950s, coming of age in a suburban Rhode Island town. In retrospect, I knew almost nothing of my parents' lives then. I would be an adult before I knew my father had spent two years of his adolescence unable to see his mother, even though she lived in the same city. But I knew that my father once had played freshman football and baseball in college, knew that my mother once had been a high-school basketball star on Cape Cod, had spent winter nights taking a boat to away games on Martha's Vineyard and Nantucket. I knew that they played golf together on Sunday afternoons, and that my mother played golf on many summer mornings, would practice hitting shots in the backyard with plastic golf balls. I knew that with the exception of visiting

relatives the only trips we ever took together as a family were day trips to New York and New Haven to see college football games.

So it's not surprising that sports became a way of life early, changing sports with the seasons. I was one of the youngest kids in town to make Little League, and brought to baseball a passion that bordered on fanaticism. I pored over baseball magazines, lined my bookcase with baseball cards, played whiffle ball against the side of the house, went searching for pickup games. On winter nights, I threw a ball across the room, aiming for my pillow. I played endless games of catch in the backyard, sandlot games in the neighborhood, listened to Red Sox games through the static. I cherished my first Little League uniform, treating it as if it were some family heirloom. By age ten, I was a starter on a Little League team named after a local factory that made lace, one of the few industries in the town. The next year I made the All-Star team and at twelve was named the Most Valuable Player in the entire league. For this I was given a small black trophy with a statue of a baseball player on the top of it. I put it on my desk in that autumn of my first year of junior high school and stared at it endlessly while supposedly doing homework.

Playing sports was fun, certainly more fun than anything else. I didn't have any other interests. No fishing, or camping out, like some kids in the neighborhood. No woodworking, or fascination with cars and the mysterious engines under the hoods that made them go. No stamp collecting or other hobbies. Nothing. Just sports.

In my little corner of the universe, sports were the way masculinity was defined. Being good in sports made you accepted in ways that being good in other things did not. It got you approval from parents and other adults. It got you approval from other kids in the neighborhood. Kids who were not good at sports got picked on; kids who were, did not.

This realization started very early, as soon as you started playing neighborhood games. The strongest kids, the fastest kids, the kids who were the best at games were the ones looked up to. Not the smartest. Or the ones who did the best in school. It was a lesson I learned as early as the second grade, when I used my baseball ability to be accepted by a group of cliquish kids from another neighborhood, kids who had little to do with me before. Later, in Little League, it was even more apparent. Adults went to the games, circled the field on playoff nights, patted you on the back when you did something well.

And everyone looked up to the local coaches. They were role models before we knew what the word meant. Their rules were absolute, unquestioned; if they told us to jump we asked how high. Even as young kids, we all knew the names of the high-school coaches, knew that Mr. Ainsworth, the longtime high-school gym teacher, called everyone "clobberheads," and made you scrub parts of the gym floor with a toothbrush if he caught anyone walking on it with street shoes on. Coaches had a certain status teachers did not have.

This was all taking place in Barrington, a sleepy little town about ten miles south of Providence on the road to Newport, a town in the midst of a transformation from small town to suburb.

It's a town that lies on a peninsula that juts out into Narragansett Bay. It's bordered by water on virtually three sides and by East Providence to the north, a low-lying area of marshes, estuaries, two rivers, and big shady trees. Barrington was incorporated in the early eighteenth century, first belonging to Massachusetts before becoming part of Rhode Island in the mid-1700s.

And where once Barrington had been a half hour away from Providence on a country road, now a new highway brought Providence closer, making Barrington an attractive bedroom community, a little hideaway of about 13,000 people on the bay with clean air and good schools, a place where in the late fifties you could go to bed at night and leave your doors unlocked, a place where trouble was some kid hot-rodding down a tree-lined street. A place where people came to forget their small beginnings and dream of larger futures.

Certainly my parents had begun that way. They had married in Idaho where my father was stationed during the war and had come back to Providence's leafy East Side to one upstairs room in my paternal grandfather's house, before moving to the suburbs and the American Dream, an old wooden brown house with a front porch one block from Narragansett Bay to the south. It was about a mile from the center of town where there were two gas stations, two drugstores, a church, and a small shopping center. No one ever called it downtown. It was "the Center," had been built in the late 1940s, and at night the older high-school kids would park their cars there and wait for something to happen, a party, some excitement, something, anything, a suburban version of waiting for Godot.

It was an era of Sadie Hawkins dances and homecoming queens, of poodle skirts and penny loafers. Of men who came home from working in Providence to water their lawns in the soft twilight, and women who always seemed to be home baking cookies from Betty Crocker recipes. No one had ever heard of cholesterol. No one's parents were divorced. Whatever social problems there were were kept hidden behind the manicured lawns and the doors of the well-lighted homes.

I didn't know about Beatniks, or the House Un-American Activities Committee, or the "red scare" in Hollywood, or any of the fissures running underneath the placid surface of American life. Occasionally, there would be something on the television news or in the newspaper about "sit-ins" in the segregated South, but in a town without any blacks, all of this might have been happening on the far side of the moon as far as I was concerned. And if somewhere there were people in Barrington starting to question the values that ran through the town like sedimented rock, not only was I unaware of them, I never saw any evidence of it.

"The times they are a-changin' "?

Not in Barrington.

Not then.

Instead, there was a sense of optimism, the feeling that you could grow up to be anything you wanted to be, an unquestioned belief that the future always was going to be a beautiful summer morning. When I was a young child, my mother would take me down to the beach at the end of the street, point across the bay to Warwick, and tell me, "I could swim to the other side with you on my back if I had to."

I never doubted her.

She also thought of herself as an athlete. She wasn't someone who stayed at home baking brownies or took any great delight in being a homemaker. In high school she had wanted to go to college in Boston to become a physical-education teacher, but her parents had sent her to secretarial school in Providence instead, where she eventually became player-coach of the girls' basketball team. She was in her thirties before she

ever started playing golf, but once she started she was serious
about it. She always was tinkering with her swing, hitting
plastic golf balls in the backyard or going to the driving range
to hit buckets of balls.

It wasn't until years afterward that I came to realize how
unusual it was to have a mother who thought of herself as an
athlete, especially in an era when women athletes were rare.
She had been the club champion at the country club for three
years straight when I was a kid, and I used to caddy for her a
lot in those days. The caddying started when I was eleven,
and lasted six years. Eventually, I came to know her swing better than she did, could tell her what club to hit, how far to the
left a putt was going to break. At an age when many other
kids began to feel alienated from their mothers, unable to relate, I was her biggest fan.

We lived in an old neighborhood in an area dominated by
many summer houses that traditionally had been rented by
Jewish people from Providence. It was between the two points
that jutted out into Narragansett Bay, the two most prestigious addresses in town. To get to elementary school I walked
past the woods across the street from my house, past the
cemetery, down a hill, and past more woods. The next year,
the bulldozers came and cleared out the woods across the
street. Soon the houses came: big, new, pastel Colonials,
houses different from the rest of the neighborhood. This was
happening all over town. Barrington was growing up with
me. It's conjecture who turned out better.

Running west of the Center was Maple Avenue, an inap-
propriately named street about a mile long. This was Barrington's Italian section, a little sliver of working class tucked
into the middle of a burgeoning suburban town. Many of the
families living on Maple Avenue had been there for genera-

tions, their ancestors once coming to work in the now-defunct brickyards at the turn of the century. Tightly knit, ethnic, many of the families interrelated, the Italians viewed themselves as separate from the rest of the town, resented "the Americans," as they called them, for moving in and taking over their town. They ran the shops, built the houses, performed the services for a community that was becoming more and more commuter-oriented. They were the kids I caddied with at the local Rhode Island Country Club, which looked majestically out over Narragansett Bay to the south, a private club that excluded Italians.

Sports were the only thing that bridged these two separate cultures, the only common denominator. Which is how I met Mike Raffa when I was eleven years old. He was the catcher on a rival Little League team, small, wiry, dark-haired, one of those scrappy little kids who always seem to make up in hustle what they lack in natural ability. Even at eleven there was a hunger about him, some burning need to use sports as a vehicle for social acceptance in a town where Italians were the "niggers," discriminated against, looked down upon.

We met one summer morning while caddying together and became instant friends, a bond formed by the respect we had for each other as Little League players. Raffa lived on Middle Highway, the main road perpendicular to Maple Avenue, in a one-story white frame house.

The first time I visited, it was like being in a foreign country. There were religious statues on the walls. The center of the house was the kitchen, dominated by a large table in the middle of the room. The living room was off one side. There were three small bedrooms off the other.

Eventually, his cramped house would become like a second home to me, his mother forever giving me plates of macaroni.

In the insular world of the Italian community I had achieved a certain acceptance: I was Raffa's friend.

His mother had grown up in Barrington, one of nine children, the daughter of a dairy farmer who had been born in Italy. Mike's father had grown up in Providence, also first-generation Italian. Both of his parents had quit school to go to work—his father in the sixth grade after his own father had died—and both viewed work as being important, not education. So Raffa had started caddying at Rhode Island Country Club while in the third grade, caddying being a rite of passage for virtually every Italian kid in Barrington. They would sit on benches under a big Copper Beech tree in front of the white stucco clubhouse, the designated caddy area. They weren't allowed in the clubhouse, save for the hallway that went by the pro shop. They weren't allowed on the veranda in back of the clubhouse that looked majestically out over Narragansett Bay. They weren't allowed in the pool area where the snack bar was. In a club where there were no Italian members, and only a couple of Catholic ones, the message was that they were socially inferior, second-class.

It also was a message Raffa got at home. He was forever being told he wasn't like "the American kids": didn't have as much money, didn't live in the kind of houses they did, was different in some fundamental way. His father didn't want him playing sports; to Raffa's father, sports were a waste of time, a road that headed nowhere.

To Raffa, though, sports were the only thing that made him feel he had value. It was a lesson he'd first learned in Little League, and then in the sixth grade when he'd been bused to a school outside of the Italian section. Sports had been his validation, the passport to acceptance, and he played them with a burning intensity, as though his whole being hung in the balance. I needed basketball for an identity. He needed it for everything.

He started playing pickup games with a bunch of us over off Rumstick Road, a long street under a canopy of elms that led from the Center to the monied homes at the end of Rumstick Point. It was there, in Jay Sarles's backyard, that we established our own unofficial pecking order.

Sarles was lean and quick, wore glasses that gave him a sort of bookish appearance, a curious mix of athlete and academic. He always got all A's in school, and one of us would invariably say, shaking his head heavenward at the apparent incongruity of it all, that Sarles was the only one anyone knew who, when faced with the choice, would rather read the book than see the movie.

By the ninth grade Raffa, Sarles, and I were the three best players in our grade, and I had quit playing baseball and football to concentrate on basketball. Which was a big decision, one that my father tried to talk me out of. It was still the age of the three-sport star, the high-school athlete who moved through the different sports with the changing of the seasons. No one at the high school seemed to play only one sport then. The best athletes seemed to play everything, the same kids in different uniforms. It was expected.

But basketball had a built-in advantage: you could play it by yourself. And I did. Hour after hour. Day after day. Sometimes it seems as if my entire childhood was spent in the driveway behind my house where my parents long ago had put up a slightly bent orange hoop. It was a driveway that served many roles, part sanctuary, part escape, a launching pad for innumerable fantasies.

While my brother Geoff, only a year younger, listened to Elvis records, snuck cigarettes, hung out in the Center with his friends, a suburban childhood out of some Norman Rockwell magazine cover, I shot baskets by myself in the backyard. At night I'd carry a flashlight through the backyard, place it against a rock so it illuminated the basket, and shoot in the dark, the thumping of the ball and the clanging of the rim the only sounds in the residential quiet. When it snowed I shoveled the court. When it was bitterly cold and the long gray New England winter with its unrelenting leaden skies froze everything, I wore a mitten on my left hand, keeping my shooting hand free.

If all that time had been spent practicing the piano I might be in the concert halls of Europe now.

It was not.

It was spent in the driveway, playing imaginary games in my head, games in which I always won with some last-second heroics. Two nights a week I went to see the high-school team play, intoxicated by the cheers, the crowd, the excitement that ran through the packed gym like an electric current. It was all there: the blue championship banners on the walls, the frenzied cheerleaders in their blue-and-gold uniforms, the crowd that seemed to be a living, organic thing. The stars of the team became my personal heroes in ways that the Celtics—playing only an hour and a half away in Boston, and the very best basketball team in all the world—never were. I knew where the high-school players lived in town. I knew who their girlfriends were. I imagined them living always in some suspended state of grace, an exalted status conferred by playing basketball for the high school. Sometimes I would see a couple of them in the drugstore in the Center. You could buy an ice-cream cone for a nickel and watch them lounging at the counter like stars in their own movies. I never doubted for a second that I would one day become like them; never doubted that my destiny was to play on the varnished court of Barrington High School beneath all those blue championship banners and hear the cheers of an adoring crowd. At fourteen years old, in the ninth grade, that was all I wished for.

Basketball already had become an obsession. Friday-night dances, called "canteens" and held in the third-floor gym at Leander R. Peck Junior High, were mostly spent talking about sports. They were our first forays into dating, these canteens were. Early in the evening the boys stood on one side of the darkened gym in the required sports jackets and ties, the girls on the other in dresses, and we viewed each other from a distance that seemed as awesome as the Continental Divide as the record player blared out "Stagger Lee," "Donna," "Don't Be Cruel," and a hundred other teenage anthems of unrequited love. Later in the evening, smelling of Old Spice, we would head across the floor in the spirit of Columbus heading off to some strange, new world.

Mostly, I stayed in the corner talking about sports. Sure, I wanted to dance. Sure, I wanted a girlfriend. But I didn't have that kind of confidence. Instead, I stayed in the warm, safe cocoon of sports-talk with the boys. Once I got to be a player, a star no less, then I would get the girl. I knew then that it was all interrelated.

By this time school was little more than something you had to sit through before practice started. Uninterested, unprepared, surrounded by classmates who had no more interest or attention than I did, we all played out this educational charade. There was Ancient History, there was the beginning of algebra, there was Latin, there was English. But what I remember most was staring at the clock, waiting for study hall, waiting for lunch, waiting for practice to start, so I could run and sweat and be comfortable again. Waiting.

The school was in the center of town, next to the town hall and the library, on the state highway that went through Barrington on the way to Warren. It was dark, gloomy, full of long corridors, and presided over by a tiny martinet of a man and his assistant, an embittered old termagent who carried a tape measure through the corridors with which to measure the length of girls' skirts.

The gym was a small bandbox on the third floor. Under one basket was a stage. Three rows of wooden chairs circled the court. During games, played on Tuesday and Friday afternoons after school, kids ringed the court, crowded on the stage, wedged between the mats that hung suspended from the far wall, screamed and yelled at the opposing team. They were the enemy. We hated them. No doubt the feeling was reciprocal.

I started on the junior-high team that year, saw my name in the school newspaper, tiny articles that I cut out and pasted in my new scrapbook with the black cover. I relied primarily on my outside shooting ability, honed from all those long hours in the driveway.

It was all a little mysterious, this shooting ability. Some games I was "on," other times nothing I shot seemed to go in. It was unpredictable, out of my control. This ability to hit shots from far away was like a gift that only showed up on special occasions, and when it wasn't there I was like a salesman with an empty sample case. On those times I almost moaned out loud in frustration. If my shots weren't going in, there was nothing I could do about it. I was powerless. This ability, this gift if you will, was so capricious, came and went so ephemerally, that I had become a victim of it. And those times when it wasn't there, I wondered if it ever was going to come back, if it would be my cruel fate to throw up shots that always hit the rim and bounced away. At those times I yearned for one more summer, so that I could revisit the private world of the driveway. I'll practice more than ever, I'd tell myself, slumped low near the end of the bench, removed from the game. I'll practice so much that I'll never miss again.

Just one more summer.

Becoming a player is a long, drawn-out process, one that takes place over many years. I was never the most talented player in Barrington. There were always quicker kids, kids who jumped better, who seemed to have more physical gifts for the game.

But becoming a player is not just about talent. I knew at a very young age that success in sports is fragile; the line between who makes it and who doesn't is thin as mountain air.

How did I know this?

I suppose I knew it from Little League, and the MVP trophy that sat on the desk in my room. I knew it from all those signs on the locker-room walls. Knew it from those stories I had read about athletes and how they had to overcome adversity, stories I carried with me as surely as I did my telephone number. From an early age this all became an article of faith, part of the way I came to perceive the world. Success in sports did not just happen to you. You had to sacrifice for it. You had to lust after it.

So I would go to games, watching better players and trying to copy them, learning some of their moves. Watching how they get their shots off, and what slight feints they made to get around their defender. How they used a screen. How to play two-on-two. I would go to games and watch these things, study them, then try and go out the next day and incorporate them into my own nascent game.

My parents started taking me to Brown games when I was

about twelve. We would sit in the few rows of bleachers underneath the basket, so close you could almost reach out and
touch the players. I saw Chet Forte play for Columbia. Years
later, he would become the director of Monday Night Football, then fall into a widely publicized gambling addiction.
Back in the winter of 1957, though, he was one of the best college players in the country, battling a Kansas sophomore
named Wilt Chamberlain for the national scoring title, a quick
five-foot-eight kid who used to shoot running one-handers
off the wrong foot. I saw John Wideman of Pennsylvania, one
of the first black players in the Ivy League, who grew up to be
the writer John Edgar Wideman.

It also was the era in which Providence College was making the transformation from a small Catholic school nobody
outside of Rhode Island had ever heard of, into a basketball
powerhouse fueled by a young coach named Joe Mullaney
and some players who later would go on to become famous.
Among them were Lenny Wilkens, a great NBA player who
coached the '96 Olympic team, and John Thompson, the longtime Georgetown coach. I listened to their games on the radio,
visualizing the action, as they introduced a generation of
Rhode Island kids to college basketball.

But even in those games in junior high when I was shooting well, I wasn't much of a player. I had trouble shooting on
the move. I didn't drive to the basket well. I didn't handle the
ball well. I certainly wasn't strong. My defense was virtually
nonexistent, a matador forever waving after some passing
bull. I played because of those times when my outside shots
went in. This was what made me different, what set me apart
from the other kids. And at the tender age of fourteen I knew
that this one ability, this gift I couldn't control, would determine my future.

But I got lucky.

In the summer before my sophomore year in high school I grew six inches, to about six foot one. No longer was I merely some little kid who could shoot the ball well from the outside. In the small world of basketball in Barrington in the early 1960s, now I was a big kid who could shoot the ball well.

I also was fortunate that I had friends who shared my interest in the game. The solitary hours in the driveway evolved into pickup games around town. Day after day we played on Sarles's court as I began to grow and develop other parts of my game. Raffa and I played basketball every day throughout that summer. We caddied at the Rhode Island Country Club in the morning, then played pickup games against older Italian kids in the humid afternoons, our bodies drenched with sweat.

Raffa and I were opposites as players. I was bigger, by far the better shooter. He was better at everything else. At ballhandling. At passing. At defense. He also knew the game better. He saw the entire court, was conscious of where his teammates were and what they were doing. He knew that being able to see the floor and passing were his niche, what set him apart as a player. I only saw the game in a straight line: my man, the basket, nothing else.

"You've got to drive more," Raffa said. "Keep people honest."

We were sitting on the ground beside an asphalt court in West Barrington, having lost a pickup game, sharing a big bottle of Coke. Our opponents had been older, more physical than us. I hadn't played well. My outside had not been falling, and during those times it was as though I didn't have any game, would never be a real player. At such times I wondered why I even played basketball, so convinced was I that I never would be any good.

"Use more fakes," he said. "Try and get your man off balance. You're too easy to guard."

Raffa was frustrated. He had to win, even pickup games. To lose was to have no value, to be just another Italian kid in a town that said that he didn't really count.

"Fake more," he said, when it was our turn to play again. "If you get them off balance, they can't guard you."

We were playing Tony DeSpirito, one of Raffa's cousins, and a guy named Frank Palumbo. Both once had played for the high school, now were about twenty years old. They drove big, hot cars with fins, cars that had fuzzy dice hanging from the rearview mirrors. They were burly and played with long pants and undershirts on, loved to beat us and gloat about it afterward. It was their way of keeping the young turks in place.

"You guys should go on spaghetti diets," Palumbo said, muscling me out of the way for an offensive rebound. "You're too weak."

But Raffa was too quick for them. Time and time again he beat his cousin off the dribble, drawing us even. And on the last point of the game, I had the ball, Palumbo came running at me, knowing I was going to take an outside shot. Only this time, I pump-faked him, and as he went running by I scampered in for a game-winning layup.

When the ball went through the net, Raffa ran over and jumped in my arms as though we had just won the state tournament.

I began to use pickup games to work on my weaknesses. Sometimes, I would try to drive to the basket every time, instead of shooting from the outside. Sometimes I'd try to dribble left-handed. Anything to become more multidimensional as a player.

Eventually, Raffa and I learned to play well together, our games complementing each other. He passed, I shot. He knew that if my man was playing me tight, I was going to fake cutting to the basket, then come around Raffa for the ball, all the while using him as a screen. I knew that he wanted room to be able to take his man to the basket, that he tried to avoid taking outside shots whenever possible.

I could feel myself improving, growing as a player in small increments, handling the ball better, acquiring the beginnings of a sense of how to play.

Other kids went sailing, or went to Barrington Beach, only a few blocks away from my house.

I rarely did.

Nor did I play golf, tennis, or participate in any of the other summer activities in Barrington. I did not hang out in the Center or spend a lot of time listening to rock 'n' roll records. I did not have a girlfriend.

Instead, I went looking for pickup games. Or else I shot by myself in the backyard, the *slap, slap, slap* of the ball against the asphalt the soundtrack to the summer. I sent away for a body-building course, complete with color-coded charts, and I did an endless succession of exercises, charting my meager progress. On soft, warm evenings, I ran with bricks in my hands through the cemetery down the street to build up my skinny arms. I drank endless milkshakes, mistakenly thinking that extra weight would help. I jumped over an old sawhorse in the backyard trying to improve a vertical leap that was almost nonexistent.

Most of all, I dreamed of being a better player.

• • •

Steve Cronin's way of selecting his team was very simple.
Players he knew went to one end of the court and were on the
varsity. Players he didn't know went to the other end and became the junior varsity.

"And if you don't like it, go home and watch cartoons," he
told one kid who didn't think he was getting a fair tryout.

Cronin was the coach at the high school, a redbrick,
sprawling school a decade old that was in the northern end of
town, at the beginning of the highway that led to Providence.
It was a school out of some suburban kid's dream, surrounded
by spacious green athletic fields. Behind the fields was the
Barrington River and a white church with a steeple. On brilliant autumn mornings, the leaves in full stage-dress, it was
possible to sit in a classroom and look at the white church, its
steeple alabaster against the blue sky, and believe it was inch-
ing closer to Heaven.

Cronin was a former Marine who supposedly had gotten
half his face blown off in the Korean War. But if he no longer
was in the Corps, the Corps was still in him. After road games
that we won he would wait until everyone was in the yellow
schoolbus, cheerleaders in the front, the players in back, and
then, with his long gray coat and scarf wrapped tightly around
his neck, eyes hidden behind dark glasses, he would march
Patton-style up the steps and into the bus while everyone had
to stand and sing the Marines Hymn. Cronin appreciated
good theater.

He taught history in a classroom with cinder-block walls
covered with maps. More specifically, he barked history.
He spat out a Gatling-gun array of facts and dates that we
were expected to regurgitate on tests. His students sat Marine-
stiff in their seats, almost at attention, as he talked about

American history from a perspective slightly to the right of Genghis Khan. Or else we gave "oral reports," as he sat in back of the class diagramming basketball plays. With roughly twenty-five students, oral reports could last for weeks. Then back to barking out facts until he could assign more oral reports.

He also was notorious for taking care of the players in his class. A few years earlier, when he'd also coached baseball, guiding Barrington to one of the worst records in the school's history, one of his players supposedly wrote "Third Base" on his final exam, leaving everything else blank. Legend had it he got a B.

"Okay," Cronin said, taking out his grade book at the end of every marking period and calling kids to his desk. "Ninety-five . . . ninety-three . . . eighty-four . . . eighty-nine . . . one hundred . . . ninety-six . . ."—before pausing dramatically— "B," as the kid walked timidly away from the desk.

Then it was a player's turn. Seventy-five . . . eighty-two . . . seventy-six . . . seventy-two . . . eighty . . . seventy-nine . . ." A pause for effect. "B."

Often he stood in the doorway hidden from the corridor.

"Watch me catch a couple," he'd say to the class. "You, you, and you," he'd growl out into the corridor, pointing at a few miscreants scurrying down the hall. "You know there's no running in the corridors. Come in here and sign up for detention."

He also refused to open a window in his classroom, and on winter afternoons, his room could become stifling.

"Mr. Cronin," a girl asked timidly, "could you please open a window just a bit?"

"What?" he boomed in his drill-sergeant voice. "And get a draft on one of my players? Show a little consideration. America didn't become great because people were always thinking of themselves, you know."

One day at practice he told a kid to take his shirt off, to play on the "skins" team. The kid struggled to get his shirt off, turning something that should only have taken a few seconds into a production. Cronin and the entire team watched as the kid continued to struggle.

"You know something, kid," Cronin finally said. "I hope that sometime in the future, under very different circumstances, you'll be able to get out of your clothes a little quicker."

The previous coach, a learned, soft-spoken man who looked like everyone's favorite grandfather, had guided many successful teams in the past, had developed a sort of tradition. The blue banners on the walls of the gym were a testimony to him. To Cronin they must have felt like an accusation. He had been struggling along for a few years now, beating the bad teams, losing to the good ones, getting by with his bluster and the often-overpowering weight of his personality.

Raffa, Sarles, and I were placed on the junior varsity team, the traditional landing spot for all sophomores. The jayvees were coached by Tom Burns, a math teacher who taught fundamental basketball and looked at Cronin with detached bemusement. As soon as the games started, it was apparent we were too good for other jayvee teams. Playing before the varsity games, we won easily, were rarely even tested. All the while, the varsity struggled. A veteran team, dominated by Italian kids who had won the state Class C football title, it was becoming obvious they were more comfortable in shoulder pads.

"Why don't you start breaking in the kids?" Burns asked.

"Can't do it, Tom," Cronin said. "The town would lynch me. I got all high-school heroes here."

I was still skinny and gangly, regardless of all the weight training and milkshakes. But I was getting better. Burns made me concentrate on defense, taught me how to play without the ball, to cut for the basket when my man was guarding me too closely instead of standing around getting frustrated because I couldn't get a shot off. He was the first coach to have confidence in me and because of that, for the first time, I began to have confidence in myself as a player.

By the middle of the year, Sarles and I were dressing for the varsity games, the biggest honor a sophomore could hope for from Cronin. Immediately after the jayvee game was over we rushed to our lockers and put on shiny blue warmups with gold trim, then ran out onto the court to join the varsity in the pregame layup drill.

One night, the varsity had a big lead at the end of the third quarter and I got into the game, scored eight points. The next morning was Saturday, but I jumped out of bed at six-thirty to get the morning paper from the doorstep. There it was, buried deep in a box score: "Reynolds, 3–2–8." Three baskets, two free throws, eight points. It was the first time my name had been in the Providence *Journal*. I saw it as passing a barrier, my career now lodged on a different level.

I also saw how people related to me differently, everyone from other kids to teachers to janitors in school. I had now acquired a certain status. For the first time it was assumed I would start on the varsity the following year, would actually become everything I always had hoped for all those nights spent dreaming on the driveway.

The following Tuesday night we played an away game at Scituate, a small rural town in the western part of the state near the Connecticut border. After a big jayvee win I was in my customary seat near the end of the varsity bench. Once again the varsity was struggling. They were mediocre at best, full of athletes rather than basketball players, primarily playing because they were older and more physical than we were, not necessarily because they were better. Somewhere in the second half, Burns, who doubled as the assistant varsity coach, motioned for me.

"You're going in the game in a minute," he said softly. "Don't be nervous. Take your shot when it's there. They're really packing that zone in and we need to make a couple of outside shots."

I breathed deeply. *Stay cool,* I told myself, *this is it.* Seconds later Cronin told me to stand up.

"Shoot the ball, kid," he said. "And don't choke."

Everything was faster, more frenzied than I was used to, the players bigger, the ball a little too new and shiny, the game a world of swirling colors, and a crowd that seemed to be a living thing, rising out of their seats in exultation, groaning with despair. Scituate was in a zone defense. We came down the floor to attack it, me on the left wing about twenty feet from the basket. The first time the ball was passed to me I quickly passed it back out to the top of the key. But the shot had been there. I had seen it.

We came back down the court again, only this time when I got the ball I quickly shot it, trying to make sure I followed through, ended with my wrist bent downward, as if my fingers were going to fit in the basket. And in that moment when the ball seems to hang suspended in air, no one knowing if it will go in or not, including the shooter, I saw it begin its downward flight to the basket. It looked good, soft as a feather in a gentle breeze. *It's going in,* I thought, *it's going in.*

It didn't. It spun out. Shortly afterward the horn sounded and I was taken out of the game. But I felt strangely triumphant as I walked to the bench. It had been close.

I first met Karen on the bus coming back from that game.

We had managed to win, had sat on the bus waiting for Cronin to make his grand entrance, had stood up and sung the Marines Hymn as he came aboard.

She was sitting in the seat in front of me, and turned to say I had played a good game. She was a cheerleader, a senior, two years older. She also was smart, attractive, and popular. All the things I wasn't. Her picture dominated the high-school year-book that year as if it were a personal album. She had enjoyed a high-school career that most kids would have given a few years of their lives to experience.

We talked for more than an hour coming home that night on the bus. I was oblivious to everything else. That someone like her, someone so completely out of my reach, would want to talk to me was the biggest compliment any girl had ever given me. By the end of the bus ride I had fallen in love. Which, of course, went unrequited.

But for the next few months, I sat in my third-floor room at night under the guise of doing homework, the radio turned down low, staring out the window. The ritual was always the same. She would turn onto the street in front of my house, drive down a couple of houses and turn around. By this time, knowing it was her white station wagon with the wood trim, I already was running down two flights of stairs, grabbing my coat and heading out the back door to meet her by the side of the house. Night after night, with the air pouring off nearby Narragansett Bay getting warmer, and the radio in that spring of 1961 playing "Blue Moon," "Runaway," and "Running Scared," I sat by the window and waited for that white station wagon with the wood trim.

While I had had a couple of girlfriends before, they had been nothing more than someone to "make out" with, that goofy little euphemism we used to cover our limited range of sexual experience. Sex was still something mysterious, easier to brag about with the boys than actually participate in with girls. School dances that year were still mostly spent in the corner with the guys. I would sit there in the darkened cafeteria as *"I'll love you forever, don't forget me ever"* created a mood as suffocating as a blanket, and would yearn to become a better player. *Next year when I really make the varsity. Next year when I become somebody. Then it will all be different.* I believed this with an unwavering faith.

Karen changed all that.

What I gave her was more uncertain. Now I can see that beneath the glittering surface of her high-school career, she was lonely, sensitive. Her older sisters no longer lived at home. Her parents were older. Her boyfriend was off at college somewhere. In a sense I became a surrogate little brother, a friend, although I certainly didn't realize that at the time. I thought it was love.

On those nights when I met her by the side of the house, we rode through the town, down the silent streets, feeling like we were the only two people awake. She told me about her fears of going off to school in September, of leaving home, of starting a new life. I talked of basketball. About how I desperately wanted to be a good player. Leaving home, going off to school somewhere, all seemed light-years away.

In June, her boyfriend returned home from college. The rides by my house stopped. Still, there were nights I sat by the window half watching for her car, remembering what she had told me on one of our last nights together, a time when my fears of the future were particularly pronounced.

"Everything is all ahead of you," she said. "You are going to be a big star and all the girls are going to be dying to go out with you."

I wasn't convinced.

2

Cronin called me into his room one afternoon after school in September of my junior year. It was one of those New England autumn afternoons out of a picture postcard. He was sitting in a back desk, glasses on the tip of his nose, peering over scribbled pieces of paper.

"Here it is," he said, motioning me to a nearby chair. "The Walking W."

He handed me a piece of paper. It meant nothing to me, a mishmash of diagrams, broken lines, chicken tracks in the snow.

"Can you visualize it?" he asked, an ecstatic gleam in his eye. "No one will be able to stop us. I spent all summer working on it. Locked myself up in the barn every day. Because this is it. This is the year we're going to get the flag."

"Getting the flag," Cronin's euphemism for winning the championship, had become his obsession, his personal white whale. There had been too many almost years. Almost good. Almost winners. Almost champions.

"This is it," he beamed. "Our new offense. The Walking W."

It really was little more than than five guys having designated spots on the floor, all of which had certain rules. Player A could only move to his right. Player B was never supposed to go to his left. No matter that this conflicted with the proper way to play basketball. Cronin's coaching creativity never had been burdened with the rigid requirements of textbook technique. The year before, he had devised a defense where his three best defensive players always were on one side of the court, the weaker two on the other. His premise was that the three players always would be on the same side of the ball. If the ball moved from one side to the other, so would the defense, the three players merely interchanging with the two. The only problem was that since the ball can move quicker than players, everyone bumped into each other in a futile attempt to change sides.

"Coach," said one distressed senior at halftime. 'People are laughing at us. Every time the ball comes toward us, it seems like we're running away from it.'"

Cronin was nonplussed.

"Hey, if you palookas are too stupid to do it right, we'll junk it. No problem."

So I really wasn't too concerned with the Walking W. Regardless of the terminology used, Cronin's offense always seemed to consist of putting the five best players on the court and essentially letting them play, unencumbered by a lot of set plays.

In fact, the Walking W became history in the fifth game of the season. We were 4–0 at the time, off to the best start in years, and had traveled to Providence to play Hope, a large city school that was the defending state champion. They were two classifications in size above us and played in one of those old dark gyms that were so much a part of inner-city schools in the early 1960s. Hope's leader was a skinny black kid named Al Lopes, who would go on to play at Kansas with Jo Jo White on a team that came within a game of going to the Final Four. Lopes was six foot six and silky smooth, and we had no answers for him. They were ahead by ten points at halftime.

Cronin was beside himself. He fumed outside the locker room. He came in and stalked in front of the metallic green lockers. He gripped a rolled-up program in his hand and kept slapping it into his other palm. Then he began talking in a strange, detached voice, as though he were reciting a poem to a seminary class. Instead, it was a lament for the Walking W.

"It's a great offense," he said, his eyes growing misty. "It could have revolutionized the game."

He hesitated.

"But it's too complicated for you palookas. Too sophisticated. You palookas can't handle it."

He paused, looked away, before turning back to us, his voice louder now. "So we'll junk it. Go back to the Basic."

That the Basic wasn't really all that different was irrelevant. The Basic sounded . . . well, too basic. "The Walking W" resonated with mystery.

We lost anyway.

But we went on to win ten straight games after that night, developing into a cohesive, explosive offensive team, regardless of what Cronin called the offense. And like all great teams, regardless of the level of competition, we had the right mix of players. Raffa was the clever little play-making guard.

He rarely shot, ran the team, always got the ball to the open man, played defense with all the tenacity of a terrier snapping at your pants leg. He dove on the floor for loose balls, antagonized opponents by constantly talking to them, ridiculing them. He was our visible emotion, our inspiration. Sarles was the other guard. Quick, smart, a good shooter, adept at slithering through defenses or using his speed to get out on the break, he did a little bit of everything, our best all-around player. Bob Schmidt was the six-foot-four center, a rawboned senior with few offensive skills who loved to rebound. One game, while we were in a zone defense, the man on his side kept making open 15-foot jumpers.

"Bouncing Bob," Cronin yelled at Schmidt at halftime. "Go out and guard him. He's killing us."

"I can't guard him and rebound too," Schmidt yelled back. "Which one do you want me to do?"

Cronin looked at him like he was crazy.

The following year Schmidt came home from college at Christmas with hair down to his shoulders. No one had seen that around Barrington in the early sixties. He said he was a philosophy major, talked a lot about Nietzsche and Kant and other names none of us had heard of.

"Who do they play for?" Raffa muttered.

Schmidt spent a lot of time in working-class bars in Warren, the neighboring town to the east, asking tired old men if they liked their lives. We all thought he was crazy.

But that winter when I was beginning to play out all my adolescent fantasies, Bouncing Bob wore green Shetland sweaters, tan khaki pants, Bass Weejuns and white socks, and went searching for every rebound as he later went searching for the meaning of life. I think he was probably more successful as a rebounder.

At one forward was Frank Eighme. He was a six-two senior with wide shoulders and enormous hands, our most dominant player, the only returning starter from the year before. He was the only one on the team who could dunk, a rarity then in Rhode Island high-school basketball. He lived in the same neighborhood as Sarles, had all but grown up on Sarles's court. All year long he and I ran neck-and-neck for the Class C scoring lead. Every Tuesday and Friday afternoon I checked the paper to see where I was in the scoring race, then cut out the article and pasted it into the scrapbook that was growing with each week. I was now six-three, still thin but no longer as skinny, still mediocre in most aspects of the game. But all those nights in the driveway were paying dividends. Now there were nights when I thought I couldn't miss, and my good shooting games began to pile up on one another.

So we had a team of role players, long before it became fashionable in basketball. Two scorers, one from the inside and one from the outside, a passer, a rebounder, and Sarles who did a little bit of everything. Not really by design, but by the good fortune of having players whose individual games meshed with each other.

Sarles also was the steadying presence, no small thing on a team. Any team is an assemblage of personalities and different egos. All teams are fragile, capable of self-destructing due to bad chemistry. We were no exception. Eighme and Schmidt were seniors, viewed this as their team. Especially Eighme, who had started the year before and had his own basketball aspirations, wanting to go to Princeton. Now they were assimilating three juniors into the starting lineup, including one whose personal game revolved around taking long shots and a lot of them. So there were times when I knew Eighme thought I shot too much, or that Raffa passed me the ball too much. But these were on the court problems, the inevitable frustrations that occur over the course of any season. They didn't extend off the court.

And Sarles was the great pacifier. He made sure everyone got along, understood each other's strengths, and in the process we began to come together as a team.

We also had paid our dues. No one had taken the summer off. No one played football. We all had run cross-country in the fall, Cronin demanding that every basketball player play either football or run cross-country, one way to keep us away from "the skirts." We all wanted to do well, and Cronin worked us hard in practice. Cronin knew our potential.

We began rolling over teams in our league, not just beating them. Winning by thirty and forty points. Five straight. Eight straight. Cronin could almost smell the flag, and as we continued to win his obsession grew.

"I'm going to bring the flag into my room," he said, in reference to the blue banner symbolic of winning the championship. "Hang it on the wall over my desk."

One afternoon he saw me talking to a girl in the corridor before practice.

"Keep your hands off my players," he snapped at her. "I know what you're after."

Cronin saw conspiracies everywhere. Whenever we went to some other school to play, he invariably thought the other coach had bugged our locker room. When an unfamiliar face peered into practice one afternoon he went red with rage.

"Scout! Scout!" he screamed, pointing to the face in the window of the doors that led from the gym to the main lobby. "Get that scout out of here."

He also was obsessed with neighboring Warren, in particular, their coach Tom Duffy. A member of a well-known

Rhode Island sports family, Duffy's announcement as coach
had received a column in the schoolboy sports section of the
Providence *Journal*. Cronin always referred to Duffy as
"Uncle Tom," although none of us knew why.

"Uncle Tom got a column when he got hired and I got two
inches next to the tire ads," he said.

On the day we were scheduled to play at Warren, the
biggest game on our league schedule, Cronin was particularly
hyper. We were both undefeated in the league. Warren was the
defending Class C champs, and the flag hung on the wall in
their gym, the flag Cronin now so openly lusted for.

The game also was fueled by class distinctions. Warren was
a working-class town full of a hodgepodge of ethnic groups
who looked across the Barrington River and saw green lawns,
comfortable homes, and Country Squires resting in driveways.
They called Barrington "Mortgage Hill," thought everyone
was rich, and saw every win over us as a triumph for egalitarian democracy. The only people in Barrington they thought
were all right were the Italians, but even they must be a little
suspect if they lived in Barrington.

We, in turn, saw Warren as low-rent, full of greasers. From
the Gothic factory that was the first thing you saw when you
crossed the bridge into Warren, to the storefront in the center
of Main Street that sold "hot wienies" and always seemed to
have a central-casting collection of lowlifes hanging outside.
We considered Warren the armpit of the world, even worse
than Bristol, our other big rival, which was on the other side
of Warren. To us, Warren was full of "mondoes," the name
we gave to kids who wore pegged pants, black boots, and
wore their hair swept straight back. In our closed view of the
world, mondoes didn't go to college, liked to work on cars,
liked to fight. To be a mondo in Barrington was to be a social

leper. And if they were mondoes to us we were "college" to them, not college, but *colleege,* with our brown loafers, chino pants, and button-down shirts.

We hated them. They hated us. Football games always were followed by victory parades through the losing town, fender-to-fender caravans full of screaming and gloating kids. It wasn't whether you won or lost but how much you could rub it in afterward. Invariably, these victory parades were met by a barrage of eggs.

Ill feelings had been heightened the year before during the jayvee game. Undefeated at the time, we were in a close game at Warren that was being played with all the finesse of a cock-fight. There was a rule that said jayvee games must end by seven forty-five so that the varsity game could start by eight o'clock. Leading by two points at seven thirty-five, the Warren jayvee coach called a time-out. When it ended he called another. The clock moved inexorably toward seven forty-five. As soon as the second timeout was called, Raffa walked over into Warren's huddle and began clapping in the coach's face.

"Great move, coach," he said, continuing to clap. "Great move, you stiff."

A Warren kid pushed Raffa. Raffa pushed back. Like spontaneous combustion, both benches emptied. Within seconds there were police on the floor as people exploded out of the stands. Within minutes everything calmed down. But it was seven forty-five, the game over.

"I always said Warren has no class," Raffa said, kicking the wastebasket as he came into the locker room.

Now we sat in the locker room before the game in our satiny blue warmups with the gold trim, the tension inside our uniforms.

"Think flag," Cronin said. "And remember, palookas, no fighting. Beat them in the bulbs."

"The bulbs, coach?" came a hesitant voice from the back of the room.

"The scoreboard, palooka. We'll beat them in the bulbs, then give them the teeth on the way out," putting his teeth together and raising his lips like some demented Bugs Bunny. "Just shake hands and give them the teeth."

An hour later it was Warren giving us the teeth. In a hothouse of a gym, fueled by a crazed crowd and a pep band that taunted us as soon as we ran out on the court, we came unglued. Warren outscrapped us, outfought us. It was their chance to stick it to the rich kids who lived across the river and they took full advantage of it, winning by eighteen. I ended the game with only seven points, frustrated all evening by a rock-hard kid named Don Ramsden who shadowed me all night long. It was my worst game of the season and I sat in the locker room afterward consumed with grief, feeling as if I had let everyone down.

The next morning I was so embarrassed I didn't want to go to school.

"You guys sucked," Steve Harlow said as he picked me up. On the radio were the Tokens singing "The Lion Sleeps Tonight."

Harlow lived down the street. He was a year ahead of me, played football. The year before he had arrived every morning at the bus stop with his arms loaded down with books, even though it was apparent by his struggling grades that he never looked at any of them.

"They help build up my arm muscles for football," he said.

He was an anomaly in Barrington. He quahogged in the summers. He went to cockfights in a rural town in neighboring Massachusetts. He liked to go to a diner a few miles away up on Route 6 in Seekonk, the road from Providence to Fall River, Massachusetts. One night he played "Big Bad John" on the jukebox ten times in a row until the owner of the diner came over and yanked the plug out of the jukebox.

"You guys really sucked," Harlow continued.

I had never failed so miserably before in public, never had felt so exposed, as though I now wore that big scarlet letter that that the woman had been condemned to wear in that boring book we were reading in English class.

Cronin walked around school all day, eyes glazed, vacant, one step away from catatonia. At practice he stood forlornly off to the side as we halfheartedly ran through some drills. He said nothing, a silent mourner at a funeral. Finally, he assembled us under one basket.

"The Touch," he said quickly. "We lost the Touch."

Dressed in a gray sweatshirt with BARRINGTON stitched across the front in big blue letters, he turned and threw a four-foot shot up at the basket. It missed.

"See," he said, his voice growing louder, more forceful. "No Touch. We didn't have any Touch."

He took another shot, then another. Both missed. We stood and watched.

"The Touch," he said quietly. "What happened to the Touch?"

He continued to retrieve the ball, run back a few steps, whirl around and fire up another missed shot, all the while babbling about the lost touch.

"At least he's not talking about bringing back the Walking W," Raffa muttered.

By the next game, everything was back to normal. Teams almost rolled over and played dead at the sight of us. I was the leading scorer in Class C, third in the state, averaging nearly twenty points a game. A couple of weeks later, we boarded the yellow schoolbus to go play Ponagansett, another small school in rural western Rhode Island, over an hour away. As always, Cronin waited for everyone to get on the bus before making his entrance. Actually, he waited for the starters to be on the bus. It was long understood Cronin would not hold the bus for either lowly reserves or jayvees. Legend had it that during his first year as coach he used to tell the jayvee team to be there at five-fifteen for away games then leave at five o'clock.

As always, he made a grand entrance, boarding the bus as if he were coming through the curtains of the *Tonight Show.*

"Check your stuff," he yelled. "Everyone check your stuff."

"Let's see," said Gary Conti, a little-used senior reserve who always sat in the backseat secretly smoking a cigarette and hoping the smoke would disappear through a crack in the window. He rummaged through his blue traveling bag. "Pizza, beer. Cigarettes. Yeah, I got everything."

"Make sure you palookas got everything," Cronin boomed, now moving down the aisle. "Because like all wars there's no turning back."

"Conti," he said. "How's the knee tonight?"

"If I make it through warmups, coach, it should be all right."

Cronin barely heard him, already making his way back to his seat at the front of the bus, the field general at the point. He stopped first to talk to a seatful of cheerleaders. They always brought food for the trip; Cronin always got some.

A month earlier we had beat Ponagansett 131–22. It had been during Christmas vacation, many older kids had been home from college; the gym, as always, was packed. We sensed they were there for a show, and Ponagansett, a new regional school in their first year playing organized basketball, was the perfect victim. We scored at will. Cronin kept the pressure on. We beat them so badly there were letters to the

Providence *Journal* chastising us, appropriately so, for rolling up the score. This was followed later by a front-page feature about a Ponagansett player shooting baskets in the dark on the farm after practice, his head full of dreams of retribution.

So we knew the upcoming game was a joke. Ponagansett was a good hour away, through Providence and out to the western part of the state. To us, it was the sticks, some foreign outpost that we made fun of. We laughed on the bus, sang songs off-key. Cronin sat in front of the bus and fumed. Later, in the new cinder-block locker room, he was still irate.

"I saw it happen in the war," he began, emotion dripping from his voice. "Guys would come into a clearing and think they saw dead Japs lying all over the place. And then do you know what they'd do?"

I didn't, but I knew it was going to be good. Cronin's pep talks always were good. I brought the white towel I had in front of my hands over my face. Across the room Frank Eighme was doing the same thing. Bite into the towel and stop from laughing. Everyone else was staring the floor. The room was tomb quiet.

"Do you know what they would do?" Cronin asked again, pausing for emphasis.

No one said a word.

"They would go look for souvenirs. Something to bring back for the wife and kiddies. And do you know what happened?"

He paused again, the room still.

"THEY NEVER CAME BACK," he yelled. "Those bodies were booby-trapped. THEY NEVER CAME BACK!"

He hesitated. When he spoke, his voice was calm again.

"It's the same way out here tonight. This is a booby trap. So don't stand around and look for souvenirs. Because if you do we will never come back alive. . . . Make them remember they're farmers."

The game was anticlimactic. We won by about sixty.

Afterward, back in the bus, the Marines Hymn having been sung, Cronin sat in the front of the bus eating more food he had gotten from cheerleaders. Another battle had been won. There were no casualties. "The Duke of Earl" reverberated through the bus. Cronin was happy.

So was I.

The season was becoming everything I always had known it could be, the playing-out of all those childhood dreams conceived on those cold winter nights in the driveway with the flashlight aimed at the basket: the excitement, the cheers, my name in the paper, swaggering down the school corridors like some rock 'n' roll star.

Basketball fever was sweeping through the school, complete with signs on the walls and pep rallies. A math teacher came to practice one afternoon to relate how he'd written the names "Frank, Jay, Bob, Mike, and Billy," on a geometric set and out of 100 students 99 identified them as the basketball team. The incredulity in his voice was not for the 99 who knew, but for the one who didn't.

At this point, school was only something to be endured. Boring English classes with endless repetitions of "will" and "shall," tedious selections from *Silas Marner*. Time in class was spent looking at the clock, counting down the minutes. Chemistry was even worse, taught by a rumpled older man who looked as if he'd been in the school for a hundred years, in a dark, shades-drawn room with the smell of Bunsen burners coming from the back and a chart full of symbols hanging over the blackboard in the front of the room. I might as well have been taking nuclear fission. Midway through the winter,

I didn't even know what "valances" were, the starting point
for doing any equation. Without them the problems were impossible. I sat in the back trying to hide behind the kid in
front of me as the teacher asked questions in class. Friday
mornings the teacher would be wearing a shiny blue suit. By
the end of the class it was smudged with yellow chalk from
leaning against the blackboard. We always had a pool going,
betting on the exact minute he would first lean back against
the blackboard. It was the only thing that kept me awake. I
got a D only because he didn't give F's.

If I never had been a dedicated student, now I was even less
so. Where once I had read books voraciously, now I read virtually nothing except for *Sports Illustrated, Sport,* and basketball magazines. I believed that being a player had to
monopolize all your time, that the very act of thinking about
other things, doing other things, having any other interests,
somehow detracted from being a serious player. Sometimes I
wished I could go home at night, sit at that unused desk in my
room for a couple of hours, then arrive at school bright and
chipper the next morning with all my homework assignments
done. I knew that was the way it was supposed to be, what
college was all about. It was in all the articles I read in sports
magazines about college athletes. After practice they went
to the library and studied. That was what I had to do if I
wanted to get into a good college, a fact my father never let me
forget.

The only problems I ever had with him were over grades.
Every report card was a battle, him ranting about how I never
would get into a good college, me being repentent, vowing to
study, buckle down and try harder, do better.

For this was the age of the Conant Report and other ex-
posés on the supposed ills of American high schools, the con-

sensus being that American kids didn't work hard enough. My father certainly agreed.

Why wasn't I studying harder, he wanted to know. Why wasn't I doing better?

My father believed that the key to the good life only fit in the door of a good college. He had gone to Brown and carried with him, however submerged, the elitist belief that to go to a state university was nowhere. "Cow colleges," he called them. He believed that if I didn't go to an Ivy League school I was headed for a life of deprivation.

At the time I figured it was because he had gone to Brown and that everything had worked out for him. It was only years later that I came to understand that everything hadn't. Although he later sold real estate in Barrington, most of his working life, along with his two brothers, had been spent running his father's small trucking company in Providence, working long hours that saw him leave the house every morning at 6 A.M. and return twelve to thirteen hours later. He never talked much about it. I was so immersed in my own life I never asked. Later I came to realize that, although the money was good enough to live in a comfortable house in Barrington, he always had been haunted by roads not taken.

The one thing he impressed upon me back then was that you had to have a "good job." Just exactly what that meant was never defined, though I eventually began sensing his wasn't it. He often talked about a college friend who worked for the Atlantic Refining Company and lived in a big house out on Rumstick Point. He had a "real good job," my father would say, no doubt wishing that instead of hustling in a small family business under attack in the early sixties by a changing transportation industry, he, too, had capitalized on his Brown degree and traded his diploma for the supposed security of a large corporation.

Surely this is what he wished for me. No matter that I couldn't have cared less, that my vision of the future stopped at next week. Even college, now less than two years away, seemed to lie out there on some distant planet. My father knew better. You can do well in school, he told me, you have the ability.

But it had already had passed me by. The truth was that I no longer could do better. Subjects like algebra and chemistry with their heavy emphasis on math were too far gone. Some nights, usually after one of my father's pep talks, I climbed the stairs to my room determined to make some sense out of my homework. I might as well have climbed those stairs to write an aria. Subjects depended on building blocks, a foundation I'd been neglecting for years. After a few minutes I knew it was hopeless, and would lie on my bed and flip through the pages of my scrapbook.

It was late February, a few inches of snow on the ground. It was still winter, but already the light was beginning to change, no longer dark by five in the afternoon. We often would come out of practice in the gathering dusk, the air still thin and cold, scrambling for rides home.

The season was entering the last week of the league schedule. We were still one game behind Warren in the standings, courtesy of our loss there. If we didn't beat them in the return game in our gym, there would be no flag.

The afternoon of the game we gathered in Cronin's room after school, our big game ritual. We sat in movable chairs and Cronin talked. Halfway through a sentence he noticed Eighme hadn't shaved, traces of red spreading over his chin like bougainvillea.

"Big Frank," Cronin said. "This isn't the House of David."

There were giggles, quick looks at one another. House of David? What was he talking about?

"Okay," Cronin continued. "Everybody pay attention and push back the chairs. We're going to change the defense."

"Change the defense?" Conti whispered. "Hours before the game? Why not bring back the Walking W and fuck everything up?"

"Forget Chico," Cronin said. "Let him waltz around with the ball. It's 'Our Hero' who puts it in the bulbs."

Cronin had names for everyone. "Chico" was his name for Warren guard Charlie Andrade. "Our Hero" was Rick Bettencourt. Del Martin was "The Animal." And, of course, there was "Uncle Tom."

"Eat something good," said Cronin. "Eat something a tiger would eat."

I ate doughnuts. One night the year before I had eaten doughnuts before a game and went out and shot well. One small bag of white, powdered doughnuts. Now it was part superstition, part ritual. As was selecting my game socks. They had to be white, long, able to reach midcalf. At least two pair. Sometimes three. They had to be worn with white, low-cut Converse sneakers, called "Cons." Nothing else. No P. F. Flyers. No Keds. Only Cons. But the socks were vital. That Christmas my mother had asked me what I wanted. "White socks," I said.

There were other rituals. The socks had to be stretched as far as they could go, the shiny blue warmup suit taken from the equipment room.

Minutes before the game, hearing the crowd noise from the jayvee game, we squeezed into the trainer's room, a small room dominated by a training table and a whirlpool.

"This is it," Cronin said. ".Lose this and it's kiss the flag adios."

We huddled together, hands joined in a show of athletic solidarity. Then a moment of silence. Praise the lord and kick their ass. With my hand in the middle of the group, I thought of all the people who had helped me be a player, my own little extended family: the guy who used to work with me at basketball camp, to an older kid in the neighborhood who used to shoot with me in the driveway. I said their names silently over and over, a personal mantra, as if by saying their names their spirits would somehow become part of mine and help me elevate my game. I vowed not to let them down.

"Okay," Cronin whispered. "This is it. The flag."

We lined up in the hallway. It was almost seven forty-five. The buzzer ending the jayvee game sounded, and moments later the jayvee came through the double doors into the hallway, faces flushed, yelling encouragement, urging us on. Electricity seemed to run through the hallway. We heard a thunderclap of noise as we burst through the double doors, running through a gauntlet of cheerleaders, their blue megaphones forming an archway. The gym already had been sold out for two hours, the crowd like kindling waiting for a match. My throat was dry and I felt out of breath, my body on emotional overload. I had this feeling before every game, the feeling that I wouldn't be able to move, a feeling that would start to evaporate a few minutes after the game started.

Cronin's new defense was resembling the Walking W. Left to dribble around and look pretty, Chico was slithering his way through our porous zone defense for easy shots. Again, we seemed a step slow, continually being beaten for loose balls. Warren was not as talented as we were, but they were scrappier, played with more of a sense of urgency—tough, working-class kids who hated everything we represented to them. At other end of the floor, Warren's aggressive man-to-man defense once again had us rattled, had taken us out of our offense, a replay of the first game. At the end of the half, we were trailing by four.

Midway through the third quarter, Warren went ahead by eleven. Raffa was beside himself with frustration. He was our emotional catalyst, for if we all wanted to win, he needed to win.

"Come on, Chico," he yelled at Andrade.

"Come on, Del, you cockhead," he yelled at Martin.

He stuck his face in Martin's face. Martin glared at him. Raffa stayed right there, chest out, jaw out, taunting Martin. Raffa had grown up hearing that Warren was tougher than Barrington, full of hard-nosed kids who wouldn't back down to anyone. He wasn't going to back down to them, ever. Even in a street fight, Raffa would have had no chance against the bigger and stronger Martin.

"Hit me," Raffa taunted. "Come on, hit me."

The gym was in pandemonium, the two referees trying to keep the game under control.

Cronin called a time-out.

"Calm down, palookas," he said, his face flushed. Our cheerleaders were on the court in their blue uniforms, but we couldn't hear them because the gym was too loud.

I had lost all concept of time and place by now, even the score. I was riding on pure adrenaline, off on some emotional high. Similar to the first game against Warren, I had been been frustrated for three quarters, followed all over the court by Don Ramsden who seemed to live inside my uniform, just like he had in the first game. He bumped me when I cut through the lane. He dogged me step for step. He was physical with me, and I didn't do well with that. I liked playing against zone defenses where I could get my shot off without someone in my face, not being shadowed by someone whose breath I could smell.

But I finally hit a shot, then another. And another. Suddenly, my confidence was back. Raffa would come across half-court dribbling the ball. I'd fake Ramsden as if I was cutting to the basket, then come back around Raffa, get the ball, and shoot it. From twenty feet away. From twenty-five feet away. It suddenly didn't make any difference. They all went in. I hit one shot falling away in the deep right-hand corner, Ramsden's hands in my face the entire time. I hit another while falling down, seeing the ball go through the basket as I lay spread-eagled on the floor, the gym a madhouse of noise. I could see Ramsden's frustration, for he had come to sense what I already knew: that it didn't matter what he did anymore, that I was going to make shots and there was nothing he could do about it.

It was as if I were in a trance, off somewhere in a private world: just me, the ball, the basket. As though the game had become a newsreel that suddenly had been slowed down. It no longer mattered where I was, or who I was playing, or what the score was, or any of it. The ball would come to me, I would shoot it, it would go in. Over and over. As if this had become my destiny, all the practice and all those driveway dreams, all the wishing and hoping, bringing me to this one place in time.

It would happen again several times in the future. From out of nowhere, for some reason, this strange sensation would come over me during a game, a sense of time being somewhat altered, a feeling that whatever I threw up at the basket was going to go in. Years later, hearing people talk about satori, about Zen masters who stare at a wall for years waiting for that one transitory moment of pure insight, I knew what they meant.

But with only three minutes to play, Warren still led by eight, sparked by Ramsden and Bettencourt who we couldn't stop inside. Our season was about to go up in smoke. But then we ran off twelve straight points to eventually win 68–63.

I had scored twenty-one points in the second half, almost all of them in the fourth quarter.

The season had been saved.

We were set to play Warren in a playoff game at East Providence High School, a large gym that could handle the expected big crowd. The only problem was that Raffa's mother didn't want him to play. He had received a couple of death threats, the phone ringing for a week, often after midnight, voices on the phone saying that if Raffa played, someone would get him.

His mother was terrified. She wasn't too keen on all this sports stuff anyway, and now there were people threatening her son in the middle of the night. Raffa had become the lightning rod for a rivalry that had gotten out of control.

"Are you going to play?" a kid asked Raffa in homeroom.

"Does a bear shit in the woods?" he said.

Warren had only lost one game the entire year; we had lost just two. They were favored, due to the fact that they had beaten us easily in their gym and had led most of the way in ours. The East Providence gym was jammed, people standing everywhere, the air full of tension. Barrington versus Warren. Rich versus poor. Mondoes against colleege. Class warfare on a high-school basketball court.

Once again the game was a rock fight, both teams clawing

at each other. Once again Ramsden was in my face, giving me nothing. He never said anything on the court, was never dirty like some guys who always tried to give you cheap shots whenever they had the opportunity. Just tough. I had come to have tremendous respect for him, to realize that in some strange way you could be linked with an opponent as well as with your teammates. I knew both of us now shared something special.

In a sense, we all had come to feel that way about Warren. They were as good as we were, and when we played each other anything could happen. We understood that great teams also need great opponents.

In the third quarter, the game was still tied before we started to pull away, eventually winning by fifteen. I had a decent game, scoring sixteen points, and Eighme was dominant, scoring twenty, outplaying Bettencourt underneath, never an easy task.

But Raffa was the star. In the last quarter, with Warren trying to press, we were trying to control the clock, and Raffa usually had the ball. This was Raffa at his best, in the open court, controlling the ball, using his quickness. He was continuously fouled. He went eight for eight from the foul line, finished with sixteen points, the best game of his career. And when he came over to the bench in the closing minutes of the game, he threw his fist into the air as the crowd behind our bench rose to salute him.

We were the Class C state champions.

Cronin would get his flag.

Now the excitement kept steamrolling as we entered the state tournament. Every game became more important, bigger crowds, more interest throughout town. Each win also became the excuse for mammoth parties, wild open houses where there was enough booze to satisfy a labor-union picnic, raucous parties that lasted into the wee hours of the morning.

Even now, so many years later, I see that week clearly, outlined in neon. The third week of February 1962. School vacation, three big playoff games, victory parties after each game. Parties that became, in a sense, my coming-out. Since each class had its own social hierarchy, I rarely had any interaction with those members of the senior class who, for whatever reason, had been anointed as the Chosen. Now that all changed. We all were on everyone's guest list, stars of the moment. We came into parties floating on a wave of good feeling.

And just as I knew all those nights sitting in the corner during junior-high canteens that one day the golden girl would come if I only became a good enough player, that, too, was starting to happen. For if Gatsby had believed that you got the golden girl with silk shirts, palatial West Egg mansions, and party music that never went out of tune, I knew you got her by being a player. Give Gatsby his green light; I'd take my jump shot.

3

Her name was Dinah.

Not only was she a senior, she also was in a group the high-school gods smiled favorably upon. It was rumored to be a fast crowd, complete with late-night parties and drinking, and the word was that Dinah didn't have any trouble keeping up. I didn't think I was that quick. I felt much more comfortable at practice than I did at parties. It was one thing to stroll through the corridors and flirt with somebody, or smile across a classroom, quite another to actually ask someone out on a date. Several times I had come within a whisker of asking a red-haired girl in my class if she wanted to go to the movies in Providence, which was the ultimate in dating in Barrington. Once I even followed her down the corridor giving myself a pep talk along the way, something about when the going gets tough the tough get going, but when I finally tapped her on the shoulder and she turned around, I asked her if she had gotten the homework assignment instead.

One of the postgame parties was at Dinah's house, a rambling old brown house in West Barrington, a solid middle-class area that somehow was different from other parts of the town that were more upper-middle-class. Class differences in Barrington were subtle. By the time we got out of the locker room and over to her house, the party was crowded, the energy turned up to high voltage. Dinah was understandably nervous. Giving a party was never without risk. Already someone had put her cat in the oven and turned the oven on.

"Can you help me get rid of these beer cans?" she said late in the evening. It was after midnight, most everyone had gone, the detritus of the party all over the living room. The kids who were left stood in the kitchen, drunk, the conversations getting louder, the stories more boisterous. The script was always the same: Soon there would be an argument, stronger words that would lead to near fights.

"Come on," she said, grabbing me with one arm, Raffa with another. We drove about a mile down Washington Road in Raffa's white Rambler, turned left on a wooded street. Up ahead was Echo Lake, a small pond really, bordered by the eighth hole of the Rhode Island Country Club. We threw the bag of beer cans in the woods. Raffa began driving back. Dinah was in the middle. I could feel her leg against me as we drove down Lincoln Avenue, the warm flicker of lights coming from houses set off the road. Suddenly she turned and kissed me. It was a kiss that whispered a thousand possibilities, whispered promise. This was the golden girl. I was sure of it.

And it was a golden time. The state tournament was being held in the citadel of dreams for any Rhode Island high-school kid who ever bounced a basketball: Alumni Hall on the Providence College campus, home of the PC Friars who only four years before had risen from college basketball obscurity to become a basketball name in the Northeast. We were scheduled to play LaSalle, a large Catholic high school in Providence. LaSalle was two classifications larger than Barrington—a school with a great athletic tradition, the kind of school we weren't supposed to be able to play with. Their team was led by Davey Lopes, who would go on to play second base for the Los Angeles Dodgers and hit home runs in the World Series. We were huge underdogs. Class C teams were almost always guests that left the state tournament early in Rhode Island.

"Don't let any of this go to your heads, you palookas," Cronin warned us in practice the day before. "Forget all that crap you read in the papers. Don't read those rags."

Two hours later, after practice, Raffa saw Cronin slinking out a side door, a blue baseball cap pulled low on his forehead, his feet hidden by galoshes. He had recently moved out to central Massachusetts somewhere, more than two hours away on slippery country roads. No one seemed to know why. A couple of nights a week, he would jump into his gray Dodge Dart and, as if the whole town of Warren was in pursuit, head off for the north country, only to return the next morning, bleary-eyed, cap pulled down even lower. Most nights he spent on the couch in the trainer's office. This night, Raffa saw him carrying a stack of newspapers under his arm. His picture was in it.

We beat LaSalle by seventeen points in a sold-out Alumni Hall in front of 3,300 people—the largest crowd we had ever played before.

When the buzzer sounded, Cronin burst out of his seat onto the court and jumped into the arms of Eighme and Schmidt, the two seniors, forcing them to carry him off the floor. The lead picture the next day in the Providence *Jour-*

nal's afternoon paper was of Cronin being carried off the floor on the shoulders of his players, as jubilant fans swarmed around him.

Now we were only two games away from being state champions, an unbelievable thought just a couple of months earlier. Our record was 22–2. We already had become the Cinderella team, the little Class C school that had ambushed LaSalle, and now we were after Rogers of Newport, another large Class A school. Cronin became more paranoid with each practice.

"The Touch," he screamed one afternoon after a period of particularly sloppy play. "We've lost the Touch again. TWO LINES . . . BACK TO THE BASICS."

We got into two lines, did a simple layup drill over and over. Back to the basics, as Cronin darted back and forth in his gray sweatsuit screaming about winning the state flag.

"You are going to play the biggest game of your lives tomorrow," Cronin said to me afterward.

He was in the small coach's office that looked out over the court. It was a small room, full of scrapbooks and memorabilia. Cronin was still in his gray sweatsuit with the blue BARRINGTON stitched on the front. I had talked to Cronin one-on-one a couple of times, felt uncomfortable around him. Cronin was a little intimidating, a little too bizarre for me, with his one-liners and bluster, even if we all knew it was a show. I was much more comfortable with Burns, the assistant coach.

"I don't want you to think about next year," Cronin said. "No one knows what's going to happen next year. So let's win now. Let's win now and we'll put that flag up and no one will ever take that away from all of us. Not ever."

• • •

Strangely enough, I remember little about the game itself. I remember the seven yellow buses that left the high-school parking lot behind us for the ten-mile trip to Providence, seven buses full of singing students and blue banners. The stuffiness of the locker room, the nervous sweat, the disoriented feeling as we ran out on the court through the gauntlet of microphones—I remember all that clearly. It's only the game that's fuzzy. Rogers was bigger than we were, a solid team with the precision of a combustion engine. Cheered by our legion of fans, whipped up by Cronin who equated the game with World War III, we were strangely flat, as if all the emotion somehow had already been used up, spent on all those big playoff games that had gotten us here. We were never really in the game, were already down twenty-one after the third quarter, then tried to hang on until time just seemed to run out on the season.

Yet it never really ended at all.

With the resiliency of youth, we were soon back playing pickup games on a court in West Barrington, down the street from Dinah's house. Already I was thinking of next year, convinced that if this year had been good, next year would be even better. Didn't all dreams come true if you only wished hard enough? Of course they did. Only the year before I had taken those evening rides with Karen, dreaming of exactly what had happened. I had led the league in scoring, third in the state, was on the all–Class C team with Eighme and Sarles. Then there was Dinah, who I now saw Friday and Saturday nights, my first real girlfriend.

The big news that spring was that Cronin was thinking of leaving. There had been too many late-night rides to his new home in central Massachusetts, too many nights spent on the couch in the trainer's office.

The other news was that I had started to be recruited by Brown, the Ivy League school in Providence, only ten miles away. Stan Ward, the Brown coach, had recently moved to Barrington, only to soon hear there was a six-foot-three guard in his new town who could shoot the ball. So one early evening in the spring of my junior year my father took me over to see him. He lived across town in a new development of pastel Colonial houses with velvety lawns. He was watering his.

"What are your boards?" he asked.

"Four-eighty in math and four-sixteen in English," I said.

He winced. "Well, the English is going to have to come up."

Ward continued watering his lawn. He was a large, stoop-shouldered man with gray hair and a bemused expression. There was also a certain resignation about him, as though there had been too many losing seasons, too many long bus rides on cold winter nights, too many years without any full-time assistant coach. Too many years of realizing basketball at Brown was always swimming against the current and there wasn't a lot he could do to change that.

"And if you're really serious, you're going to have to go a year of prep school after you graduate," he said, almost as an afterthought.

Prep school?

The last thing I wanted to be was a preppie. There were several of them around town and they were somehow different, never really accepted. Ward was going on about how since I was the son of an alumnus I would undoubtedly get some added boost in the admissions process, but that I also was going to have to go someplace where I would learn some study habits, plus get that English board score up so I might have a chance of getting admitted. It seemed far away to me, off in some distant future. All I could think of was the upcoming summer, next year. The future could take care of itself. It always had.

"Are you interested in Brown?" Ward asked.

"Sure," I said.

The fact was, Brown was my only frame of reference for what a college was. For years my father had driven me by it, told me stories about it. I had grown up going to Brown football games. Someone mentioned college and I saw Brown. The fact that it was one of the more academically demanding schools in the country was irrelevant. I never gave a thought that I might not be even close to being able to do the course work there. Didn't I have native ability? Hadn't everyone always told me that I could do well in school if I only applied myself? I even half believed it.

"Read the editorial page," Ward said. "It will improve your vocabulary."

I barely heard him. I was being recruited and I was thrilled. As was my father. For the first time, he envisioned a way for me to go to a prestige college and, ironically, it had nothing to do with climbing the stairs to my room every night carrying schoolbooks.

That summer before my senior year seems forever bathed in soft orange light. There were sultry summer afternoons, full of blue sky and puffy white clouds that would hang out over the bay like feather canyons in the sky. Raffa and I rode down quiet tree-lined streets in his white American Rambler, a car Raffa liked because he could push a button and the front seat flipped down, creating an instant bed. He said he liked to do that on first dates, liked to watch the reaction on the girl's face. We always rode by girls' houses.

"Let's check them out," Raffa would say.

And always there was talk of next year, next season. Basketball was never far from our consciousness. It monopolized our conversation, carried our thoughts. We were going to win the state championship, something no Class C team had ever done. That was our goal, and everything became geared to that. Two nights a week, we played in a Pawtucket summer league, rolled over teams.

Other nights I was with Dinah, sitting in a parked car on lonely roads exploring first love. Talking of feelings, dreams, the initial beginnings of trying to bring the world into focus. *"We learned about love in the back of the car, the lessons hadn't gone too far,"* Harry Chapin would sing a decade later. He must have been in the backseat.

After Dinah I would have many relationships, but I brought the same baggage to them all, experiences gleaned from those crazy, passionate, seventeen-year-old nights in parked cars. That wild and never-come-again time of falling in love and not knowing any of the ground rules. Never again would I feel the same urgency, the same vulnerability, the instinctive belief that it was so completely right, as I did back there in that adolescent love with Dinah. And if first love is a trip that you can make only once, I never had any regrets about taking it with Dinah. She was smart, complex, searching. In short, she was the contemporary woman just waiting for the next decade. Already, in that summer of 1962, she knew she had to get out of Barrington. I, of course, didn't understand why.

Even schoolwork was getting better while I waited for the start of my last high-school season. It was the autumn dominated by the Cuban Missile Crisis, an event we discussed daily in a course called Problems of Democracy, one of several easy courses I was taking. Since I was definitely going to prep school next year, there wasn't any reason to bury myself under some heavy academic load as a high-school senior. Instead, I took journalism, a casual early-morning class where we sat around reading the newspaper, occasionally pondering the mysteries of something called "the inverted pyramid."

There also was sociology where we read about different tribes, something designed to expand our rather myopic view of the world. Ironically, after a year of reading about all the South Seas tribes, I still thought the people from the neighboring blue-collar towns of Warren and Bristol were the strangest I'd ever seen. If the school department had offered a course in neighboring towns instead of South Pacific tribes, everyone would have been better off.

Problems of Democracy was taught by a charismatic, athletic, Irish Catholic man whose initials were JFK, initials he signed corridor passes with. The text was *U.S. News and World Report,* a magazine as politically conservative as Barrington itself, and we were assigned the back-page editorial to read every Friday, no doubt so that we would go off for the weekend armed with the threat of the Red Peril.

"You have to get tough with the Russians," he'd say, standing in front of the class, slapping a ruler against his palm. "Get tough with the Commies and they will always back down."

It wasn't a particularly overpowering course load and without the rigors of math, science, or a foreign language, I became a decent enough high-school student. For the first time since elementary school, I didn't feel any academic pressure. Not like the year before in chemistry where periodically we would sit in small groups in the lab mixing chemicals together to

produce foul-smelling milky solutions. At which point one of
the girls would invariably cover her nose and all but squeal,
"Oooh, that's gross."

The tests were even grosser. Faced with problems that
seemed as indecipherable to me as some space-age code, I
slumped in the seat trying to sneak a peek at the paper of a
small kid next to me, one of those kids who looked smart. But
like all the high-school classes I sat through, what's recalled is
vague, hazy, moments of watching the clock inexorably moving toward the time the ringing bell would save us from those
academic boxing rings where we were being routinely beaten
and battered. There were so many of these times, moments
spent imprisoned behind a desk, anxious, hoping some teacher
wasn't going to call on you and reveal the plunging depths of
your ignorance for all to see.

In a sense, I envied some of the Italian kids who, without illusions, stripped of any academic pretense, had surrendered a
long time ago.

"Mario," snapped one teacher, "if you don't be quiet I'm
going to call your parents."

Mario sat slumped in the back, dungareed, black hair
greased and slicked back. Every classroom seemed to have
them, lost kids who seemed destined to play out daily audi-
tions for juvenile-delinquent roles. Kids who spent much of
the day sequestered away in "shop courses," divorced from
the school's mainstream.

"Do you hear me, Mario?"

Mario straightened up in his seat, gave the teacher a quick
sneer. "Save the dime. Buy yourself a new suit."

Yet I also secretly envied the kids in the top classes, the kids
who always had their homework done, who had notebooks
with neatly defined sections for different courses and neat,

legible notes, and who took down their assignments in little green pads.

Somehow I had ended up in the middle, part of the school's *lumpenprole*. All of us on some conveyer belt to college without any idea what that meant. We half did homework assignments, crammed for tests, waited for the bell to ring so that we could go on to the next class and do it all over again.

The inherent futility of it all had been expressed in chemistry one morning the year before on a bitterly cold February morning, snow blanketing the football field visible out the window. Someone had asked a question about a particular way to do one of the problems.

"Which way did you do it?" the white-haired teacher asked, writing it on the blackboard.

"The first way," answered the kid.

The teacher stopped, looked back at the board. "That's the Harvard way," he said. "The Princeton way. The Brown way. You do it the other way. The simple way."

I was doing it the simple way. I was taking courses I could understand, courses predominantly filled with kids without any more academic interests than I had. Much of the time I worked on long, elaborate, rambling love letters to Dinah, who was off at a small Catholic women's college in Boston, a couple of blocks from Fenway Park. She had left in September, and although Boston was only about an hour and a half away, it might as well have been halfway to the moon. That she now was off at school in a city with thousands of college students caused an ache in my heart. I would have felt threatened if she had gone off to a convent.

So I wrote her long, long letters pledging my love, letters filled with familiar references, emotional connections that I hoped she would respond to in such a way that would cause her to look out on all the excitement and energy of college life in Boston and see, instead, a string of soft summer nights sitting in a car with me, her favorite jazz station purring from the dashboard. So I wrote her letters in hopes of reminding her. She wrote back, not as frequently, trying to reassure me. Somehow I wasn't convinced.

One Sunday afternoon a couple of weeks after she'd gone, I was riding around town with Raffa, missing her, worrying. Suddenly we were on our way to Boston, going up the old Post Road from Providence to Boston, then through Jamaicaway to Brookline Avenue and her small redbrick college alongside Beth Israel Hospital. We sat in her dormitory lounge while the front desk buzzed her room, my stomach doing flipflops, sweating, like in the locker room before a big game. What was I doing here? Why wasn't I home playing ball somewhere? Anything but sitting on some vinyl-covered couch feeling like Harry High School waiting for Dinah while several girls kept poking their heads into the lounge to check us out. Why was I wearing sneakers? Why was Raffa wearing his blue Barrington sweatshirt with EAGLES in yellow on the back? Why did she have to go to school here?

Dinah and I ended up sitting in the Sears parking lot, just down Boylston Street from Fenway Park, while Raffa took a walk. We decided that on the following Sunday I would come up for the day.

It became a weekly ritual in that fall of 1962. Every Sunday morning at nine-thirty, I got into my mother's gray Falcon with the red bucket seats—dressed in gray flannel slacks, brown polished loafers, and one of the two tweed sport coats I owned—and drove the hour and a half to Boston, feeling not unlike a young Daniel Boone heading off to the Cumberland Gap. Boston was so big, so far away from Barrington.

I always got to her dorm minutes before eleven, just in time to meet her coming back from church. The days were spent riding around Boston. She knew little about the city. I knew even less. Together, on those brilliant azure afternoons, we began discovering it together: Chinatown, the Combat Zone, Cambridge with MIT and Harvard sitting magisterially on the Charles, the monied suburbs of Newton and Wellesley. I learned about all of them that fall, driving around in my mother's gray Falcon like some fifties version of Dink Stover at Yale. The fact that no college kid was wandering around Boston on those Sunday afternoons in a sports coat made little impression on me. I wasn't going to sit around Dinah's dorm lounge in sneakers.

Her curfew was nine-thirty. That always found us parked outside the snack bar on the street behind the campus. By this time, all the reassurances of love had been given, my fears temporarily put on hold until the following week. Just what did I think this all meant? I didn't know. I wanted it to be vacation so she could come home and we could get back to normal. I didn't like her here in Boston where there were so many things to do, so many college guys walking around. I didn't want her going out, didn't want her to go to parties, really didn't want her to do anything other than sit in her room and write me letters.

So there were Sundays in Boston with Dinah, days I came to see as nothing more than keeping the lid on a relationship I sensed was about to go *poof.* And there was my life back home. Already, they were beginning to go in two different directions. There was Dinah, there was basketball, and the two didn't seem to have anything in common anymore.

Where my classmates worried about what college they were

going to, filling out endless applications, I was on a temporary reprieve. Next year I would be going to some prep school, then to Brown. It all seemed unreal.

Not that I thought a lot about it.

I lived completely in the present tense, looked at life as if it were about six inches away from my face. The future was next week, not next year.

Under the pretense of going to the library to study, I often got out of the house on school nights, spared from those nightly charades of climbing the stairs with my arms loaded with books. Located on a small hill in the center of town, adjoining the town hall, the library looked like an old New England country house. It also was the perfect meeting place.

"Let's bolt," Raffa would say, after a few minutes of our masquerading as students.

One November night, heavy with the chill of late autumn, Raffa and I drove through West Barrington, past Dinah's house, the porch light on. I wished she were home. Then I could go up the stairs and into that house and it would be like she never had left. But she had left and it wasn't the same and I didn't know why. The streets were quiet, the houses still, lights flickering through the darkness. We drove farther down Washington Road, took a left and drove by Joan's house. She was a cheerleader, Raffa's girlfriend off and on for three years. He always referred to her as a pain in the ass. They were "off" on this November night. We stopped at the end of her street. Raffa got a green trash bag out of the trunk. It was full of empty beer cans.

"What are you doing?" I asked.

"Watch," he said, throwing the Rambler into first gear.

With the headlights off, he drove slowly by her house, reached out and threw the bag on her lawn.

"That was A.C.," he said, the headlights back on. "All class."

In Raffa's world, most things were neatly arranged into two categories: "all class" and "no class." The trench coat he had begun wearing to school. The seat in the Rambler that fell back. The white socks and loafers we all wore to school every day. Chino pants and Shetland sweaters. Those were A.C.— all class. "No class" was anyone from Warren.

Girls also fell into two categories: "all action" or "no action." Except for Joan who was a pain in the ass.

Outside the drugstore in the center of town we saw Sunde and Patsie, two jayvee cheerleaders. They were known as "drive-in" girls, as opposed to girls you had to take to the movies in downtown Providence. But they weren't "scags," the ultimate female pejorative.

"What are you guys up to?" asked Sunde, who was was short and buxom and a year behind us.

"It's boys' night out," Raffa said. Ever since seeing a movie of the same name, saving one night a week for going out without girls had become one of his articles of faith, right up there with never taking a girl to an athletic event.

"Let's go for a ride," Sunde said.

I wasn't too sure. What if someone saw us? Even though I knew Dinah had all but rejected me, I didn't want to publicly announce it.

"Come on," Raffa said, as they stood on the sidewalk in their green loden coats. "You know their action. We'll take them to Echo Lake and attack them. If they give us any shit, they can walk home. What else are we going to do? Go back to the library?"

They got into the car, Sunde in the front with Raffa, Patsie in the back with me, unlike some times when Raffa tried to make the two girls sit together in the back because, he said, that's what married couples always did.

"Patsie's having a party Saturday," Sunde said. "Her parents are away, so pass the word."

Parties were becoming more and more boisterous with unlimited liquor. But I never drank any. I'd watch my friends get falling-down drunk, throw up in the street, have to all but carry them home almost every weekend, and I never once took a drink. Not out of any sense of morality, but rather from a skewed sense of wanting to be different, of being more dedicated as a player. So I sat in cars as we rode around town with cans of Narragansett, Budweiser, and malt liquor; I went to the parties and watched everyone get crazy, and I liked being there, liked watching it. No doubt there were kids who thought I was as drunk as they were. But I was a player and players didn't drink. I had read it in a book somewhere.

"Let's go park somewhere," Raffa said. "I don't have any gas."

"Let's get something to eat instead," Sunde said.

"Come on, Sunde," Raffa said. "How about a break?"

"What do you guys think we're going to do?" Sunde countered. "We're not just going to go parking."

Raffa looked like we'd just lost to Warren.

After they had wolfed down cheeseburger and vanilla Cokes at a diner out on Route 6, just over the Massachusetts line a few miles away, Raffa drove around Echo Lake, parked in a small clearing bordered by tall pine trees.

Through the trees you could see moonlight dancing on the lake. Raffa cut the engine. This time the girls didn't offer any objections. No, they really didn't want to go just yet, and it probably would be all right to park if Raffa was really sincere about saving gas. But just to talk, understand.

"What do you think you're doing?" Sunde said a few minutes later from the front seat. "Don't touch the merchandise."

"Come on, Sunde," Raffa said. "I spent a buck on you."

Sunde scurried across the front seat toward the door, running her hands over the front of her sweater. "A buck!" she screamed. "A buck! I'm worth five."

After we dropped them off, Raffa took me back to the library to get my mother's car.

"That's the trouble with skirts," he said. "You spend money on them and it's never enough."

He looked out the window into the darkness, shaking his head at the apparent injustice of it all, before turning back to me.

"No class."

The season was all-class, though. Eighme and Schmidt had graduated, but three kids were up from last year's jayvee team ready to step right in and augment Raffa, Sarles, and me. One was Pat Monti, Raffa's cousin. He played basketball with a deadpan expression and had moved into Eighme's slot as a scoring forward. Another was Steve Tilander, a skinny six-foot-seven kid still as green as spring grass, but a giant in Class C, a basketball Gulliver. The third was Joey DeSisto, talented enough to start for any other team in our league. As was Jimmy Fiedler, the quarterback on the football team. Raffa called him "WJIM" because he talked a lot, and always turned up the radio whenever Fiedler got in the car, hoping he might get the hint.

I had known them for years, had grown up playing against

them in Little League. I knew how they thought, knew their girlfriends. There was nothing they could do or say that could surprise me. I was bonded to them in ways that had become second nature. In a certain sense, I felt as if we all had prepared for this year together. Certainly Raffa, Sarles, and I had. This was going to be our year, even more than last year had been, the continuation of the story that had begun when we'd been the only three seventh-graders to make the junior-high team. We knew that this was going to be the last season we would ever play together.

Cronin also was gone. He had left with his flag, gone off to who-knew-where. The new coach was Phil Coen, a former Boston College football star, with the upper body of a weight lifter and a calm style that exuded a quiet strength. "All class," Raffa kept saying over and over. "Phil's all class."

Coen also was stepping into something of a hot seat. Last year, we had snuck up on the Rhode Island high-school basketball world. Now we were expected to win. In our minds that included the state championship, something no Class C team had ever done. Anything else would be a letdown.

Everything started according to script. We steamrollered teams in December, easily crushing schools in higher divisions. If anything, we appeared to be even better than the year before. I was scoring a lot of points, playing with more confidence, a confidence that bordered on arrogance.

"So you're the big star," an opposing player sneered at me minutes into a game, his face pressed close to mine.

"Yeah," I said. "Too bad you're not."

That August I had gone back to the basketball camp in the western Rhode Island woods for a week, a camp that included most of the best players in the state. It was run by Joe Mullaney, the coach of Providence College, and Ernie Calverley,

the University of Rhode Island coach. Both were in their thirties, still young in their careers. Both had been excellent college players themselves: Mullaney had played on a national
championship team at Holy Cross in 1947 where one of his
teammates had been Bob Cousy. The year before, Calverley
had thrown in a shot from three-quarter court to beat Bowl-
ing Green in the National Invitational Tournament in Madison Square Garden, a shot that had given him a slice of
basketball immortality.

It was my third year of basketball camp, and I saw it as
being invited into some secret society, some brotherhood of
basketball with its own codes, its own language, its own way
of perceiving the world. You could see that basketball could
be a way of life, not just a game. I returned home with both
the high-scorer and the MVP trophies. There wasn't a game I
played in that I didn't think I was the best player, at least of-
fensively.

Our first league game was against South Kingstown, the
only team in our league that had black players, although we
called them "Negroes" then. Either that or "colored." They
came from across Narragansett Bay in the southern part of
Rhode Island, played in a gym Cronin always had called "the
graveyard." When we won there the year before, Cronin had
got down on his knees and kissed the court. "I beat the graveyard," he kept saying. "I beat the graveyard."

Now South Kingstown was reputed to be the second-best
team in our league, our first serious challenge of the young
season. So Raffa had an idea.

"My house, five-thirty," he said.

His parents were out, a large bowl of spaghetti was on the
kitchen table. There were five of us: Raffa, Sarles, Monti, De-
Sisto, and me. We sat and ate spaghetti with clam sauce. Then

Raffa walked into the living room and put on a record. He called us in and turned out the lights.

"Psych music," he said, turning up the volume. It was "Climb Every Mountain."

We lay on the floor in the dark while an inspirational chorus sang "Climb Every Mountain," "The Impossible Dream," and "You'll Never Walk Alone."

"Okay," Raffa said, when the last crescendo of emotion had drained from the speaker, jumping up and down, pounding his hands together. "Let's go kick some ass."

We went north on Middle Highway, past the junior high, and took a right on Lincoln Avenue before coming up on the high school on the left. The cars were jammed along the road, spilling out from the big parking lot in the back. We walked through the winter cold and came in through the boiler room.

There were two ways to approach a home game. One was to sit in the stands during the jayvee game, then stand up dramatically during the third quarter and casually stroll toward the double doors that led to the locker room—young warriors getting ready for battle. The other was to come in through the side door and go straight to the locker room, as we were doing tonight.

I was nervous, was always nervous before a game. I had moments of panic. Suppose nothing went in? Suppose everything I shot kept hitting the rim and bouncing away? Sometimes I had such a dream, when shots would arch gracefully toward the basket only to pop out, dreams from which I would awake feeling anxious and drained.

The game was never close. We won easily, I scored twenty-six points. Most of the other games became carbon copies. We'd get big leads early; the starters were on the bench by the start of the fourth quarter. I was averaging about twenty points a game. We were sweeping through the league schedule.

Monti had settled in just fine in Eighme's spot. He was not as strong nor as experienced, but he was clever and had a knack for scoring inside. DeSisto was a great sixth man: scrappy, multidimensional, with a nose for the ball. Only Tilander struggled, not quite ready. Like most tall kids, his coordination would develop later and he would become an appreciably better player a couple of years out of high school. We couldn't wait that long. We needed him if we were going to have a realistic chance of winning the state title. Without him, we were too small.

Outside of one loss at South Kingstown when Raffa was hurt and didn't play, we only had two other close games in the entire league schedule. Even though Warren had lost Cronin's old buddies "Chico" and "Our Hero," and Ramsden, my old nemesis, was slowed by a bout of mono, they played us tough in their gym, just like always. Stan Ward, the Brown coach, came to see me play for the first time. He sat on an elevated platform in the corner, a kind of makeshift press area. I got thirty points, including twelve for twelve from the foul line, in a foul-filled brawl of a game that should have been played in shoulder pads.

"You shoot the ball pretty good," Ward said afterward in his low-key way.

Pretty good? I thought. How about real good? I was seventeen, the ball was going in, and everything was right with the world.

Bristol also was tough, another hated rival, a little town on the way to Newport, which every Fourth of July has the largest parade in the country. They played in a small, dark auditorium across the street from Colt Memorial High School, named for the family that made their fortune selling firearms and once summered on an estate along Narragansett Bay. A stage was under one basket, where kids, all wearing Bristol green, sat and taunted opposing players. Orange nets hung from the baskets, accentuating the lack of light. The visiting team's dressing room was down a flight of narrow stairs and through two wire-mesh partitions.

Bristol held the ball, deliberately passing it around the perimeter of our zone defense, sometimes for as long as a couple of minutes, before they even attempted a shot. At the end of the first quarter the score was 3–2. We were behind 8–7 at the half. The noise in the second half was ear-splitting, bouncing off the faded yellow-brick walls. The crowd, sensing the huge upset, screamed and chanted as the cat-and-mouse game continued.

Then Raffa got hurt.

He had hurt his knee the spring before, had had cartilage removed in August. It had been a long operation and he had tried to come back from it too quickly. He now played with his knee taped, but it wasn't the same. He was still quick, but he had lost a step, too.

Now he was hurt again, writhing on the floor in pain, his hands over his face, moaning. The crowd booed as he was carried off, yelled at him, heckled him.

"See what I told you about Bristol?" he said through clenched teeth. "No class."

But Sarles stole the ball and we went ahead for the first time. Now, behind by a basket, Bristol could no longer stall. Now they had to come out and play and we eventually won by ten.

Afterward, in the locker room and getting ready to go out

to the bus, four Bristol policemen came down the narrow stairs.

"We're giving you an escort to the bus," one of them said. "Some of the natives are getting a little restless. Stay together and move quickly."

"Just get on the bus," Coen said sternly. "Don't say anything to anyone and don't stop."

A crowd of people was outside the door, milling around, stretching back to the street while others circled our yellow bus. The police opened the door; we followed them quickly to the bus. Traces of old snow lined the sidewalk. All around were faces, noise, hate. Some eggs hit one side of the bus, snowballs the other. The driver revved the engine, scattering the crowd in front of the bus.

"I told you they were N.C.," Raffa said. "No class. No fucking class."

Once on the bus, we got more brave, rushing to the windows to give the finger, make faces.

I felt on the very top of the world I'd created for myself.

Outside the high-school windows, February was bright and cold, a typical New England winter. Inside was a warm cocoon of friends and a basketball season that was progressing as if I had written the script. It was everything I had ever hoped for all those nights out in the driveway with the flashlight on the basket and the glove on my left hand. Winning a game in which I had played well, surrounded by my friends who were all I ever thought I would need in the world—it was the ultimate high.

There were classmates all around me who were no doubt waiting for next year and their chance to leave Barrington, to get to the next chapter. The overwhelming majority were going off to college somewhere. They couldn't wait to get out of Barrington.

Not me.

I wanted to freeze-frame everything, live in that winter forever.

Three weeks later the season ended.

We already had won the Class C title, the second year in a row. But that had seemed anticlimactic. Unlike the year before, we now were expected to win. The goal was the state championship, not the Class C title. That had been the goal since we had lost to Rogers last year. This was going to be our time. No Class C team had ever won a Rhode Island state title and we were going to make history.

We were going to play Sacred Heart, a Class B school from Central Falls, in the quarterfinals of the state tournament. The site was the University of Rhode Island in Kingston, across Narragansett Bay from us, about an hour and a half away. The summer before, we had easily beaten Sacred Heart twice in a summer league, already we were thinking of a rematch with Rogers.

We lost by ten.

After the game, we sat around in the blue-carpeted locker room as if we had just witnessed some terrible accident. As if any moment someone was going to poke his head through the locker-room door and say, "Okay, the real game starts in a few minutes." My high-school career was over and I wasn't ready for it. It hadn't ended right, hadn't ended like I had dreamed all those long-ago nights in the driveway: the state championship, the cutting-down of the net, the cheers, the hero.

I had been awful, never really into the flow of the game, had played with the feeling that any minute I would somehow get untracked and things would be different. I had picked up my third foul in the second quarter, had to sit out for a while, something that never had happened before. My shots had gone up soft, the ball spinning lazily backward just like it was supposed to, looking good, then popping around the rim and bouncing away. Just like in those horrible nightmares. Time and time again. Or else the ball never seemed to come to me when I wanted it, either too soon or too late, somehow not right. The more the game progressed, the more frustrated I became, burying myself in a personal funk.

And where was Sarles, who had sparked us so many times before? Or Pat Monti, who had scored explosively all year? The three of us never had had a bad game at the same time before. Unlike last year, when we'd been beaten by a better team, this shouldn't be happening.

Sacred Heart?

Sacred fucking Heart?

With a couple of minutes left, I looked up at the scoreboard clock that hung suspended from the ceiling in the middle of the court. We were fourteen points down.

Over at one end of the court our cheerleaders were kneeling down. Joan Goodall, whom I had known all my life, who lived only one street over. Gail Anderson. Carol Renaud. Sue Morin. Joan, Raffa's on-again, off-again girlfriend. We all had grown up together, shared the same teachers, went to the same parties, listened to the same records, had shared a coming-of-age that we once figured was going to last forever. They, too, had a vested interest in the season, had been jayvee cheerleaders, then varsity ones. They, too, had been the stars of their class and now it was ending for them, too. They had tears in their eyes. There would be no miracle comeback.

It was over.

With eight seconds showing on the clock, Sacred Heart passing the ball around as we scurried after them in frantic pursuit, hearing the Sacred Heart crowd chant down the final seconds, I walked off the court. I went through the doors that led to a runway, then up the stairs to our locker room. The buzzer sounded and a massive cheer followed me up the stairs. But it wasn't for me.

I knew very little of my parents' lives. I did not know that my mother's father had been a bastard, had never known his real name, and had been raised by a family named Bowman in western Massachusetts. Nor did I know that my father had spent two years of his adolescence forbidden by his father to see his mother, even though she, too, lived in Providence, as part of their divorce settlement had been that my grandfather got custody of the three boys or he would not pay for their education. I didn't know that my grandfather had physically abused my grandmother, or any of the other reasons why they'd divorced. I did not know what my ethnic background was or what European country my ancestors once had come from. I did not know where my grandparents had grown up or what their lives had been like before they became my grandparents. I did not know how my parents met, or how long they dated, or much of anything about their childhoods other than that my father had played football and baseball in high school in Providence and my mother had played basketball in high school. I did not know the houses my father had lived in growing up in Providence as a child, even though I had grown up only ten miles away. I did not know which house my mother had grown up in in Falmouth on Cape Cod until I was an adult, even though I spent my childhood visiting my cousins in Falmouth.

I did not know these things because they were never discussed, and I, for some reason that now seems unfathomable, never had any curiosity, so immersed I was in my own child-hood.

My father and I related through sports. They were a safe harbor against the vagaries of family life. It had started dur-ing my Little League games. He would usually show up late in the game—still in his white shirt and tie, having come direct from work—and stand behind the backstop. He would com-municate to me in silent ways, a smile here, eye contact there, our own private code. We never communicated any better.

In other ways we communicated very little. We did not talk about politics or sex or religion or anything that might have been on the front page of the newspaper. He never asked me about Dinah. In the traditional way of American suburban life in the 1950s, my mother raised my brother, my sister, and my-self. She was the one we felt comfortable with, the one we knew loved us unconditionally. She was the one I felt I could tell anything to.

With my father, the equation changed, however slightly. There was the sense that you had to somehow win his ap-proval, that there was a right way to do things and a wrong way, one path that would take you through life: do well in school; go to a good college; get a good job. A by-the-numbers approach to success in America.

That was his message, repeated over and over again.

Not that I ever rebelled against it. It seemed reasonable enough. Yet it also was totally irrelevant. I never thought about the future, about becoming an adult, or having a career, or any of it. My vision of the future stopped with playing col-lege basketball somewhere, and even that was fuzzy, a pic-ture out of focus.

So by the time we were heading toward Worcester Academy on a cold gray morning in early March, we were comfortable within the parameters of how we related to each other.

Worcester Academy was the poor cousin to the more prestigious New England prep schools, the scruffy street kid. Instead of a sylvan woodsy setting, the school was surrounded
by three-decker tenements, sagging porches, tired old wooden
houses that needed new paint jobs. The neighborhood sat on
top of one of Worcester's many hills, overlooking a forlorn
downtown. Sports were the equalizer at Worcester Academy,
and their message to their more prestigious peers could have
been as simple as this: You may send more kids to Harvard,
but we still kick your ass. A decade later, Worcester Academy
would claim such disparate alumni as Cole Porter, Abbie
Hoffman, and baseball flake Mark "the Bird" Fidrych, who
had a brief bout of fame as the pitcher who talked to the baseball.

But the only thing I knew that gloomy March morning
was the place looked as if they could have filmed a ghost
movie there. Time-worn brick buildings circled a small tired
lawn that was brown and scruffy. At one end of the small
campus was the gym. It, too, was redbrick; it, too, was old. An
antiquated running track hovered over the court, making
it impossible to shoot from the corners. My father and I
met the coach, who talked about rules and nightly study halls
and "paying the price," and other things that barely regis-
tered. His office was cold and dark. I tried to picture myself
here and couldn't do it. I had seen a glimpse of my future and
didn't like it.

"What do you think?" my father said, as we left the campus.

"I think I should have studied more," I said.

That night Raffa, Sarles, and I went back to the University
of Rhode Island to watch the semifinal games of the state

tournament. Raffa called it returning to the scene of the crime.

He was going to go to college next year—Assumption, also in Worcester, Massachusetts—a Catholic school that had one of the best small-college basketball traditions in New England. Ever since junior high he had wanted to go to college, had wanted to one day be a high-school coach. He knew he didn't want to do the mill work his father did. In the Italian culture of his youth, he considered it important to do better than his father had done. That was the benchmark for him and the other Italian kids: Do better than your father did.

"You know," Sarles said, as we sat in the first row, the game swirling by around us, "in a crazy way I'm kind of glad it's over. Next year there won't be all the pressure to score a lot of points and win every game. Hell, we only lost two games all year and it's like everyone thinks we failed. It doesn't make any sense. Two lousy games. What about the nineteen we won? Don't they count?"

He was going to Amherst next year, had been admitted early-decision back in the fall. I had known Jay forever, as far back as the second grade, and he always had seemed to have his life scripted, always gave the impression that he had a vision of the future that I so profoundly lacked. His life always had seemed in balance—basketball was important, but not as important as his schoolwork; his social life was important, but never in the way it was to so many other kids who only lived for the weekend, as if there was no tense other than the present.

"I think I'm going to enjoy playing next year more," Sarles said.

I thought about what he said. I never had really thought about my basketball future. Everything had been geared to high school. All my hopes. All my dreams. From all those nights out in the driveway when I was a kid with the flashlight to those spring nights two years ago riding around town with Karen yearning to one day be a star. Now all that had happened. But now what? I wasn't sure. Maybe Jay was right. Could it really be any better than it was? I didn't know. But I also didn't want to think about it. It was only March. September was another world away. There was the spring to look forward to, then the summer with Dinah. After a rocky winter, when I had gone the entire season without seeing her, now things were somehow mysteriously better. She had gone out with some college guys, she said, but all that was over now— now she was convinced she truly loved me. I couldn't wait for her to come home.

The following week my father and I visited Phillips Exeter Academy in southern New Hampshire, one of the most prestigious prep schools in the country, a supposed escalator to the Ivy League. The day was bright with the first touch of spring sun, everything clear and in focus, a photograph that had been air-brushed. The campus was intimidatingly beautiful, red-brick buildings with veins of ivy caressing them, expansive lawns flanked by large elm trees that spoke of permanence, tradition. The small town served as a backdrop to the campus, like a movie set.

The coach met us, gave us a quick tour of the gym and a dorm. Kids in blue blazers and rep ties passed by with their clean-skinned faces, their hair straight and brushed. I could visualize myself studying here, buying into their long academic tradition, sitting at a varnished desk and doing my assignments in some color-coded notebook, a stack of well-sharpened pencils on one side, an eraser on the other. Not like my third-floor desk at home where I never could find anything.

The director of admissions ushered me into his office, motioned me into a captain's chair, looked at me over brown-rimmed glasses that rested on the bridge of his patrician nose. All around me were the accoutrements of what I thought was academia: bookcases that lined the paneled walls, a pipe that lay on his desk, soft rugs and chairs with school insignias on them. He asked me some perfunctory questions. I mumbled back some perfunctory answers.

"What books have you read recently?" he asked.

I hesitated. I had read one book in high school that wasn't about sports, a novel about politics in Washington that Dinah had given me.

"*Advice and Consent*," I finally said.

He nodded, continued to look at me as if he thought this was merely the first of many, a laundry list of literature.

"Anything else?" he finally asked.

I said nothing, gave a helpless shrug. What else was I going to say, *The Mickey Mantle Story*? My stomach was suddenly behind my tongue, rivulets of sweat starting to run down the inside of my arms, just like the minutes before a game.

"How about periodicals?" he asked.

I stared blankly at him. Periodicals? What were those? Periodicals? I knew it had something to do with books. Knew there was a periodicals section in the town library, the place where we all used to meet in the parking lot on school nights. But what was in it? I kept staring blankly back at him, the room full with an interminable silence.

"Magazines," he said slowly. "What magazines do you read?"

A few weeks later the rejection letter came in the mail. It didn't matter. I would be going to Worcester Academy. The year after that I would be going to Brown. It was all planned.

And I knew all about college. I had been to football and basketball games at Brown. I even had been to a fraternity there, one night when we had crashed a party, ending up in the basement bar. Next door, in a darkened lounge, couples danced to the syrupy strains of the Lettermen's *"When I fall in love, it will be forever, or I'll never fall in love."* College looked like fun.

And I knew that you got there not by what books you read, or even whether you knew what periodicals were. You got there because your jump shot went in.

4

My roommate walked in the door. He was fifty pounds overweight, lived in Panama, and had been at Worcester Academy since the seventh grade.

"Do you play any sports?" I asked hopefully.

He didn't.

It was my first day at prep school and already I wanted out, already had the sinking feeling this wasn't what I expected. My room was tiny, just big enough for two beds, two desks, two dressers. The walls were pale green, the building so old it once had been a hospital during the Civil War. It looked as if Count Dracula lived down the hall. It had towers on each end, a grim, foreboding place that matched my mood.

I already had been told the school rules by the faculty adviser, a pale ascetic who lived down the hall and spoke as if he had stepped off the pages of an English novel. Study hall every night from seven until nine-thirty, where you were supposed to be at your desk. Lights out at ten-thirty. A morning assembly every day at seven-thirty in Warner Theater, so named for one of the sons of the movie family, an alumnus. Classes until three in the afternoon. And if you didn't have a class, you were supposed to be in "the Pit," a large room in the main building with a balcony overhead where teachers watched warden-style. Jackets and ties were to be worn all day. And the one thing I hadn't counted on was that we were only supposed to be able to leave the campus two weekends a semester. I had envisioned spending weekends with Dinah, still in school in Boston only forty miles away. Now I was to be a weekend prisoner, still essentially stuck in high school while she was now a college sophomore. The news felt like an elbow to the stomach. The little world I had created for myself was now crumbling like an elaborate deck of cards left out in the wind.

I sat back on my bed and looked up at the ceiling, battling despair, trying to think of all those slogans taped to all those locker room walls of my childhood. "When the going gets tough the tough get going," and, "Quitters never win, and winners never quit"—those slogans were supposed to be the ship that got you through the rough seas, the ones that were supposed to be the foundation of my life. Now they seemed as old and useless as dead leaves blowing across a dusty playground.

I missed Dinah. I missed Raffa. I missed home. I missed everything that was familiar. Underneath the bed were two suitcases. I still hadn't unpacked them.

Every night that first week I told myself that tomorrow I would leave. Then every morning I would put on a blue blazer with the school insignia on it and shuffle off to a morning assembly where we had assigned seats and sang the school hymn, before marching across the quadrangle in search of grades and recommendations that were supposed to get us into a better college. I felt as if I were marching off to a losing battle. Every night after study hall I ran across the quadrangle into a building that had two pay telephones in the basement, my lifelines to Dinah and the world. Sometimes the pay phone on her hall was busy. Sometimes I was too late and had to sit and wait for the phone, the frustration tearing through my insides like an out-of-control virus. On such nights I would walk back across the green in the dark and climb the stairs to my room, defeated and feeling utterly alone.

Study halls were mostly spent writing long, elaborate letters to Dinah. I worked on them with the dedication of a poet, convinced that all I had to do was explain my innermost feelings, let her truly know, then surely she would love me forever. To the fact that she was involved in her own search, and that her life was as uncertain as mine had become, I was oblivious. She wrote me letters, too, but the only parts I really connected to were the parts that said she loved me, that I would always be "special," a loaded word I always ignored.

School was also more difficult than anything I was used to. From the beginning, math was a disaster, a labyrinth of sines and cosines in which I was forever trapped. On the first test I got a 35 out of 100, so hopelessly out-of-it that I didn't even know how to begin the problems, never mind solve them. I would make scratch marks on the paper then erase them, then repeat the process, all in hopes of making it illegible so that the teacher would think that at least I had started the problem and wouldn't realize the staggering depths of my ignorance. English was held in a room high up in the main building, with a view of the highway cutting through downtown Worcester, a road that I envisioned going all the way to Boston. I would

watch cars go by in the afternoon sunlight and wish I was in
them, anywhere other than sitting in a classroom listening to
a youngish teacher with smooth skin and rosy cheeks drone
on about the Victorians, his eyes fixed on the far wall.

Western Civilization was taught by a smug, red-faced man
named Munson with a tongue sharp enough to cut glass. He
was forever referring to me as "the jump-shooter from Rhode
Island." He spent the first couple of weeks showing us slides
of famous paintings "so that your girlfriend will think you're
cultured." Then he smiled, almost to himself, as if amused by
his own thoughts. "Won't she be surprised?"

I remember two things from that long-ago class, though.

"All you guys think you're cool," he said one brilliant Oc-
tober morning, the campus trees a palette of colors. "You
think you know everything. Think you know just what it's all
about. Well, someday some woman's going to come along
with a little style and you'll be traipsing after her like little
puppy-dogs."

I already knew exactly what he meant.

The second was equally direct.

"Whenever you have to make a serious decision," he said,
"make it and never look back."

Munson didn't mince many words. How he happened to
have ended up in his thirties teaching at Worcester Academy,
I never knew. He always gave the impression that he was well
aware there was a larger world just outside the games and
that he was missing it, a realization that didn't make him
happy. A decade later, in the midst of the tumult of the early
1970s, he supposedly left his wife and family and ran off with
an eighteen-year-old. I've often wondered if he ever looked
back.

At the end of the second week I took one of my two week-

ends for the semester, hopped a bus from downtown Worcester to Boston on one of those clear Indian summer mornings
that belong on a postcard. I was wearing my blue blazer over
a light-blue knit sweater. *College,* I thought. *Preppy.* Dinah
and I walked around Boston, later went to an empty apartment a friend had let her use. It was bittersweet; I was painfully
aware of each passing hour. Dinah seemed a little distant, a
picture out of focus.

"I've just been working too hard," she said. "There's nothing the matter."

I wasn't convinced. Then again, I was never sure about
Dinah. She always was brighter than me, more searching, always a couple of steps ahead.

Midway through the next week I devised a plan. A kid down
the hall had told me that if you went away for a college interview it didn't count as a weekend. He didn't have to tell me
twice. Soon I had interviews lined up at four colleges that I
had no desire to go to, spending Saturday in Boston instead.
But things with Dinah were deteriorating. Without a car, without any real place to go, an increasing tension hovered over
us. She was unhappy, she said, and didn't know what to do
about it.

One night we went to a party in a fraternity at Northeast-
ern, one that eventually culminated with the lights off and
people making out everywhere you looked, just like the parties back in Barrington. We ended up lying on the bottom half
of a bunk bed. The room was in shambles, paint peeling from
the walls. This was college? It all seemed as low-rent as Warren and Bristol. Dinah began to cry, at first quietly, then with
more force.

"You don't understand," she said, the anguish in her voice. "You never understand. You think it's easy for me around here. But this happens at every party. People pair up and end up in bedrooms. But you're never here and what am I supposed to do? Nothing is right anymore."

That's nonsense, I told her. Everything will get better. You'll see. I'll go home next weekend and borrow a car and we'll get out of the city. Get away from all this. Just you and me. Like it used to be.

The next week I was in my mother's gray Falcon with the red bucket seats, just like last year. But it wasn't last year and we both knew it. She was a sophomore in college now and I still was ostensibly in high school, fighting every weekend to get out. We didn't have any friends in common anymore, or any interests.

So we drove. Down to the South Shore, away from Boston on a chilly afternoon that smelled of winter. We drove and tried to talk, about how unhappy I was, about how unhappy she was. On the way back into the city we drove down Massachusetts Avenue, cutting through Roxbury, the Boston ghetto. All around us were burnt-out tenements, boarded-up buildings, defeated faces sitting at bus stops, miles and miles of desolation, like a trip through some Third World country, a world I knew nothing about. Dee began to cry.

"It's not fair," she said softly, and at first I had no idea what she was talking about. "The poverty. The injustice. It's just not fair and nobody does anything about it."

She started talking about SDS meetings she'd been going to, about groups like SNCC; about Martin Luther King, Jr., and racism and injustice; about civil rights. I was silent. Here she was talking about suffering and injustice, the tears running down her cheeks, and all I could think of was my own pain.

Certainly I knew that her pain and my pain weren't similar. Yet I could think of nothing to say. SDS? SNCC? Civil rights? I knew nothing about any of this. Colored people? I didn't know any. Not really. The only Negro I knew was Donald Suggs, a basketball player from Tolman High School in Pawtucket, with whom I had played on an all-star team the spring before. I had given him rides a couple of times. He never had talked of racial oppression. I told Dinah this, hoping to make some elusive point. She stared at me blankly.

"I'm thinking of joining the Peace Corps," she said later, as we sat on the lawn of the Fenway across from the Museum of Fine Arts, a few blocks away from Fenway Park. "Of leaving school. It's become very unimportant. I don't do anything. I'm just wasting my time and money. I would like to do something significant, something where I feel I'm making a difference."

"Me too," I lied. "I've been thinking of joining the Peace Corps too."

I hesitated. "Maybe we could go together."

"I'm serious, Billy," she said. "Very serious. I don't know what's happening to me, but I know I need some time to think. To be alone."

My throat started going dry, as it did minutes before a big game.

"This is no good," Dinah said, her voice small, the words sounding far away.

"But I'm miserable because I'm locked up in that school," I said. "Not because of us."

She was silent, looking off in the distance, no doubt contemplating a world that no longer included me. The late afternoon seemed suddenly colder, the dark clouds low and threatening. The day had turned sullen, as heavy as my heart.

"Well, you better start to ask yourself why, then," she said. "To find out the things that are important to you and do them."

I left shortly afterward, leaving her at her dorm, then driving off, the pent-up tears streaming down my face. Her words echoed in my mind. *Find out the things that are important to you and do them.*

Wasn't that Dinah? Maybe I would quit school and go live in Boston. Get a job doing who-knows-what, and someplace to live, and be close to her. But then what? Wasn't she still going to be miserable, crying over people in Roxbury, and talking about things I knew nothing about? Wasn't I always trying to react to her, and never really able to?

Halfway home I knew the most important thing to me: basketball. The one thing that always had given me pleasure, given me everything. The one thing I always could rely on.

The next morning, back in Barrington waiting for my father to drive me back to Worcester, I went out in the backyard with the ball to shoot baskets. Just me and the ball, like it always had been. *Forget Dinah*, I told myself, *get yourself together. Just play ball and forget everything else. Just play ball and things will take care of themselves.* The shooting eventually calmed me down, balm to my frayed psyche.

And the longer I shot in the driveway, that place that had been my first basketball universe, the more I told myself that you couldn't depend on anything. Not your family. Not your friends. Not the sense that things were going to remain the same. Nothing.

Just the game.

Sports at Worcester Academy were considered very serious. It was the way the school competed with the more prestigious New England prep schools like Exeter, Andover,

Deerfield. They had tradition, ivy-covered buildings, green lawns that whispered of a cloistered world of privilege. Worcester Academy had sports. Being good in sports was expected, an integral part of the school's fabric. It was the reason there were roughly twenty-five postgraduate students a year, most of whom were athletes. It was the reason there were so many former college athletes as teachers, men who also coached. The reason that the scores of games were read at morning assembly.

The inherent message was that academics and sports were two sides of the same coin, the mind and the body, and a *man* excelled in both. Also inherent was the message that sports could teach you things, too, lessons of teamwork and sacrifice and all those other values that coaches were forever talking about.

Donald "Dee" Rowe fueled it all. He was intense, emotional, demanding. He was in his early thirties, served as both the basketball coach and athletic director, and his pregame pep talks had become performances themselves, featuring opening acts, rising climaxes, a finale that should have been accompanied by the beating of drums.

The year before, he had given his team such an emotional send-off that one player had jumped up, burst through the nearest door, and ended up in the swimming pool instead of the gym. Dee Rowe kicked over trays of oranges at halftime, pounded the blackboard, spoke in a low voice, his face contorted in pain, spoke of all the players who had come before us and had given blood, and how could we possibly let them down? He talked about how we were disgracing our uniforms, our school, our teammates, our parents, ourselves. He made us feel guilty. Sometimes he made us want to cry. Most of all, he made us want to kick ass. I never played harder than I did that year.

At three o'clock every afternoon, we met in a classroom in Kingsley Hall, the math building behind the gym, decades of grime having turned the once-tan building almost brown. For the first half hour we were supposed to be studying, then Rowe went over strategy for the next half hour, what he wanted to accomplish in practice. More importantly, these daily sessions were forums where Rowe translated his values, time-honored verities of sacrifice, dedication, discipline, tradition.

In many ways he was preaching to the choir. We all had grown up in the age of coach as absolute ruler. Even those who were rebels at heart, or those who were the advance guard of the countercultural explosion that was only a few years away, never really rebelled. The few dissidents knew enough to be quiet about it. We had come of age in an era where players tried to act out the coach's vision, even if we disagreed with it. The questioning would come later.

We were only a couple of months away from the Beatles, the group that eventually would change the culture forever. But in those daily meetings in Kingsley Hall, listening to the world according to Dee Rowe, the Beatles and everything they would come to represent were light-years away.

"You are all part of something greater than yourself," he said. "People before you have given blood so that you can wear that uniform with pride."

Later, Rowe would go on to be the coach at the University of Connecticut, leading the Huskies to the Eastern Regionals of the NCAA Tournament in 1976 and five straight winning seasons. In 1980 he was one of Dave Gavitt's assistant coaches on the Olympics team, the ill-fated one that never got the chance to go to Moscow. In a sense it was payback; Gavitt had been Rowe's assistant at Worcester Academy the year before I got there. Rowe pushed us, prodded us, trying to make us an extension of his own vision. Every practice was timed, by the numbers. Every practice became an audition where you played for your future, for everyone knew there was talent throughout the lineup, too many players with too few minutes to go around.

Basketball again had become my life raft, the daily escape. But not without adjustments. On those fall afternoons when the leaves dripped with color, we had informal pickup games in the gym, games that established the unofficial pecking order. For the first time in years I had to prove myself all over again, this time against bigger and better players. I no longer was the fair-haired boy, the star, the one that was expected to score all the points. That role fell to Steve Adelman, a rugged six foot six, with a barrel chest and black hair that he wore swept back like some fifties movie star. Adelman later went on to become a star on some excellent teams at Boston College under Bob Cousy, the last player cut by the Baltimore Bullets in the fall of 1968. In the fall of 1963, though, he already had the physical presence of a twenty-five-year-old, and had spent one postgraduate year at Worcester Academy where the team had been New England prep-school champions. He lived two doors down from me, studied diligently, worshiped Dee Rowe, and looked at Worcester Academy as some Shangri-La that had changed his life and given him a basketball future.

Skip Olander, his roommate, also was close to six foot six, and had been there the year before as a postgraduate. He had grown up in the same Connecticut town with singer Gene Pitney, and played his records over and over. *"Only love can break a heart, only love can mend it again"* constantly came wafting down the hallway.

They were the two mainstays, befitting their status from the year before, and true believers. The rest of us were looking to fit in, struggling to find our place.

The other guard was Dick Stewart, who later would go on to play at Rutgers with Jim Valvano, and eventually become Valvano's assistant coach at North Carolina State. He was tough and tenacious and every day we played one-on-one on a side basket. Every day we battled, little miniwars that made me better.

Unlike in high school, where we basically had freelanced on offense, now there were set plays. Pass the ball to the side, then cut through. Get the ball back and swing it to the other side, then go screen for someone else. Everything was a lot more complicated than Cronin's "Walking W."

Most of the plays were designed to get the ball inside to Adelman and Olander. Plus, I also was trying to learn to play guard, the position I would have to be able to play in college, six foot three being too small to play forward. Now I was supposed to be able to handle the ball and run an offense, not just wait on the wing for someone to pass me the ball as in high school. It was all new, and there were days when the confidence seemed to run out of me as profusely as the sweat did.

There also was a seriousness about everything. Practice was competitive, demanding. Basketball no longer was all about cheers and girl smiling at you in the corridor. Everything had been turned up a notch.

My days had fallen into a predictable routine: morning assembly, classes, study hall, more classes, practice, more study hall. Over and over. Weekends I had to sign in every hour, my penance for having been caught in my ruse of supposedly going off for college interviews. I saw it as Dinah's legacy.

I was even forbidden from walking across the street to Grogan's Spa, the unofficial hangout, where in the first few weeks

I had sat at a back table and played a Tony Bennett song about how once upon a time a girl with sunlight in her hair put her hand in mine and said she loved me so; but how that was once upon a time and now the girl is gone. Every time I played the song I could feel the ache in my heart.

It was a Friday afternoon, the third week in November. Thanksgiving vacation was in the near future, I was finally playing on the starting team. The day was unseasonably warm, a pale sunlight making the old redbrick of the campus look softer. A bunch of us were coming down the stairs in the main building.

"Kennedy's been shot," someone said excitedly. "In Dallas. It's all over the radio. They think he's going to die."

It was as if everything had stopped, a photograph we were all a part of. How were we to know then that somehow things would never be the same, that something irretrievable was lost that afternoon, something precious as innocence? How were we to know that that afternoon would become the defining moment of a generation?

"You will remember this day for the rest of your lives," Dee Rowe told us that afternoon. "My generation had Pearl Harbor. This is yours."

The third game of the year we were to play the Amherst freshmen in western Massachusetts, getting on the bus in jackets and ties as Rowe sat in the front seat and watched us file by him.

"No talking," he said, standing up as the bus pulled out of campus, heading for the Massachusetts Turnpike. "We are going to war. Think about what you have to do."

Amherst figured to be an easy game. Rowe had an extensive

scouting report on them, as he had on every team. We had gone over their personnel in those daily meetings in Kingsley Hall, knew what they ran, what defenses they played, knew more than we ever wanted to know about them. I was excited about seeing Jay Sarles, who was playing for Amherst; I couldn't wait to see someone familiar, as if merely being around someone from my past might jolt my game back into what it once had been. Now I only shot if wide open—even that was tentative, so concerned I was about not making any mistakes.

I didn't make any mistakes against the Amherst freshmen for the simple reason that I didn't do anything. Just got the ball and passed it. Adelman got thirty-five points or so, no one else did anything, and we ended up losing a close game. Most of the second half I spent on the bench, frustrated, miserable, my only consolation seeing Sarles slither through our defense the way he used to do in high school. I was proud of him, as though his success somehow validated me too.

Afterward, when Sarles came into our locker room, I was still in my red uniform, utterly depressed.

"What are you doing?" Sarles said to me. "You didn't do anything out there. It was like you were invisible."

"That's the way it's supposed to be," I said lamely. "Everything is geared to getting the ball inside."

"You're a shooter," Sarles said. "You've always been a shooter. Shoot the ball and forget about everything else. Just play your game."

Play my game.

What was that? I wasn't sure anymore. It had all been so simple the year before: my game, the little world I'd created for myself, the feeling I was in control of it. Now it was all so different. School. Dinah. Basketball. Now I was like a player who didn't have a game anymore. At least not one I could trust.

Which is probably why I seemed to gravitate to the other rebels on the campus, the ones that, for whatever reason, didn't seem to fit in any better than I did. Like "Debba," who lived next door and loved to walk around the dorm in red briefs and no shirt, constantly flexing his overdeveloped muscles. He was a football player from around Boston who had taken to calling me "Weekend" ever since my ill-fated scam to escape on weekends, a story that had gained me a certain campus notoriety. Everyone thought I was crazy, which wasn't the worst thing in the world at Worcester Academy. Being considered crazy gave you a certain status, one-third of the trilogy. Along with being an athlete, of course. The third element was being considered an "ass man," although we all pretended to be that.

Debba was forever coming into my room, flopping on the bed, grabbing his crotch, and moaning, "I'm so horny. I don't think I can stand it anymore. Even your roommate is starting to look good." At which point my roommate, clad in his white terrycloth robe, would bury his head farther into a book in hopes that Debba would disappear into some puff of smoke.

But Debba was nothing like the kid who had grown up in the same town as him in suburban Boston, another football player who lived downstairs. He called himself "the Iceman."

"Because I'm cool when the heat's on," he said.

No one doubted him.

He had become so notorious on campus that kids would crowd into his room after study hall to hear him tell stories. They always were stories about the exploits of his friends and himself, stories about how he used to lift weights until he cried, until he threw up. Stories that Debba swore were true.

In fact, it was soon apparent that Debba was very deferential around the Iceman. Around him Debba didn't preen, didn't flex his muscles. Maybe because the Iceman dwarfed him, a Muscle Beach ad come to life. His upper body was so large, so well-defined, that he came through doors almost sideways, entering with a dramatic flourish. Do not fear, the Iceman's here.

He told stories about his innumerable stunts, one of which supposedly had landed him on the pages of the Boston *Record-American*. The year before, he and a couple of his buddies had destroyed a Harvard Square coffeehouse, then famous as being one of the breeding grounds for the emerging folk music scene in Cambridge, Joan Baez and Tom Rush having gotten their starts there. He walked up on the stage and began lighting the singer's beard on fire as his friends starting throwing glasses off the walls. In his words, it became "a Wild West show," tables overturned, people screaming. The next day's headline read, Coffee Club Clobbered.

Another time he had a gun that shot blanks, one he'd stolen from a track meet. He brought it into a popular bar in Kenmore Square in Boston, went into the men's room. A guy was standing at the urinal.

"Okay, asshole," he said, showing the gun. "Down on your knees. Put your face in the trough."

Seconds later someone else walked in. The Iceman duplicated the scene. Soon he had half a dozen guys all on their knees with their faces in the trough. Then he fired the gun into the air. People from all over the bar starting moving to the men's room to investigate, as the Iceman calmly walked out the door.

"You better get in there," he said, as the manager tried to push past him. "Some nut has a gun in there."

We were in the same math class. He was failing miserably, as I was. He was forever trying to cheat on tests, even going so far as to grab the test paper of some kid sitting next to him and copying it as the other kid sat there without a test paper in front of him.

The Iceman divided everyone into two categories— studpeckers and flitpeckers—and already had become a campus legend, never wearing a coat in winter, proclaiming, "No outer threads." Once he cut in line at dinner, only to have some kid complain. He quickly grabbed the kid by the throat with one hand, and lifted him off the ground as if he were a cat.

"Don't ever let me see you on vacation, flitpecker," he snarled.

Eventually, he would get thrown out of school, Worcester Academy being too small for someone who was "always cool when the heat's on." I saw him again two years later. It was spring weekend at Brown and he showed up with a friend he called Studs. The highlight of the weekend was an outdoor concert. The Iceman walked around in a black Beatle wig, a leopard skin, a skirt, and combat boots. Oh yeah. He also carried an oversized dog bone in his right hand. He patrolled the concert just waiting for someone to say something. Later that night he showed up at my fraternity, went to buy some beer tickets.

"Do you have an ID?" asked a kid we called "Hot Dog," timidity in his voice.

The Iceman grabbed him by the throat, turned him around so Hot Dog was looking at himself in the mirror.

"What do you want to see, my kid's library card?" he growled. "I don't have an ID. I'm a name brand. So why don't you take a look at your teeth before you lose one?"

The next time I saw him was nearly two decades later. I was working as a reporter in Newport, Rhode Island, sitting in the office on a summer morning. The office was on Thames Street in the middle of the tourist district and I was passing time by watching the stream of people walk by the office when he walked by. I knew it was him. I went outside and followed him up the street for a while, before tapping him on the shoulder.

He turned and looked at me a beat, before the recognition came into his eyes.

"Did you see *Animal House?*" he asked.

I thought it was a strange response to someone you hadn't seen in fifteen years, but, hey, this was the Iceman. Strange always was part of the equation.

"John Belushi had writers," he snorted. "They made it up. I lived it."

Certainly he did, back there in the autumn of 1963.

We played again midway through the following week against the Brandeis freshmen, the last game before Christmas vacation. It was an afternoon game, the little gym so loud you couldn't hear yourself think. For the first time in four years I did not start, sat halfway down the bench with my maroon warmup shirt on, trying to he inconspicuous. I felt as if everyone was looking at me, as if they all knew my failure.

Again we were struggling. Again Rowe went berserk at halftime, trying to come up with something, anything, that would get his team out of the collective funk that now seemed to be infecting everyone. We were like a high-priced engine badly in need of a tuneup, needing something to make all the disparate parts start working in precision. But what?

Midway through the second half Rowe put me in. We were down by four. The first time I got the ball I was supposed to run a play. Instead, with Sarles's admonition of *Play your game* in my head, I took two hard dribbles right and pulled up for a jump shot. The ball went in. As it did the next time I got it. And the time after that. By now the crowd that sat up on the track overhead had come alive, and the season began to change dramatically for me. For the team, too. We began rolling over opponents, never losing another game. I was scoring a lot of points, the perimeter complement to Adelman's strength inside. And with that success I started to feel better about everything, another reaffirmation that basketball was what I could depend on, the one crutch that always could get me through the tough times.

It made me forget about Dinah. It made the nightly study halls bearable. It gave me a reason to be at Worcester Academy, my world once again in focus. Once again a season had become its own reality, going from game to game; once again I was on an escalator that moved on its own power, sweeping me along with it.

The away games were the best.

It really was going off to war: Dee Rowe in the front of the bus, nobody talking, the countryside rolling by out the window. At such times it was possible for me to think that there was a world outside of the Worcester Academy gates, and that with each passing week I was getting closer to it. We traveled around to New England prep schools. Late in the season, we even went to Exeter, where I had visited the year before. We won, I had a good game, and fervently wished that the smug admissions director from the year before had seen us play.

Who gave a fuck what periodicals were?

The New England Tournament was held at Boston College, complete with the famed Bob Cousy, who had just become the

BC coach, sitting underneath the basket. I had twenty-seven points in the semifinals, even throwing in a running hook shot, the only such shot I ever made in my life.

In the finals against Maine Central Institute a few days later, I once again was in that same zone I had first experienced against Warren two years earlier. Everything was going in, time seemed altered, the basket looked as big and inviting as Oz off in the distance through the mist. I knew I wasn't going to miss, was never going to miss, not today anyway. But we were behind at halftime and in the locker room Rowe was beside himself.

"You see this ball," he said, standing in front of us in his dark, well-pressed slacks, polished loafers, white shirt, and red rep tie. "No one here wants this ball. Not one of you really wants it."

He dropped the ball, watched it bounce harmlessly to the floor, then start to roll away.

"But I want it," he yelled.

He dropped to the floor on top of the ball, hugging it to his chest, and rolled over. "I want it."

He got up, then dropped the ball again. Again he dropped on top of the ball, cradled it, rolled on the floor with it.

"But I want it," he yelled. "I want it. You may not want it. But I want it."

The emotion swept through the room like a live current, almost bounced off the walls. It was all wonderful theater, and Rowe was a master of it. We thought it was spontaneous. Years later, though, I learned it was an old trick in the city of Worcester, the favorite of Lester "Buster" Scheary, once Cousy's coach at Holy Cross, and later a sort of coach-mentor in the Worcester area, known for his histrionics as a camp lecturer and after-dinner speaker. Later that spring, at an awards banquet, Buster had delivered an overwrought wail of a speech about the country, a speech that came wrapped in Old Glory. "That's his 'I love America' speech,' " said a kid who was from Worcester. "I've probably heard it twenty-five times."

Buster's favorite ploy, though, the one Dee Rowe had so successfully borrowed during this particular halftime, was his basketball-camp routine where he would stand in the middle of the court holding a ball, then for some reason, slowly start undressing until he was down to his jock strap. By this time he would be rolling around on the court virtually naked, a white-haired man in his sixties, all the while cradling the ball, fondling it, whispering sweet nothings to it, telling everyone how much he loved the ball.

On this day, fueled by Rowe's impassioned halftime performance, we gradually pulled away in the second half. I finished with thirty-four points, one of my best games ever. Minutes later, amid the jubiliation of the locker room, the headmaster came over and shook my hand. He had a wooden leg and used a cane; his face was florid.

"Great game," he gushed. "You made us very proud today, very proud. Now we'll see about getting you into Brown."

A week later someone from the Brown admissions office called my father and said I was in.

Once again basketball had delivered for me.

The fact that I was flunking one of the four subjects I was taking? The fact that I had been been caught a couple of weeks before, plagiarizing a book report out of *Masterplots* by my English teacher, who then had written a letter to the headmaster saying that "as an instructor of integrity I don't see why I should have to have this young man in my classroom"? The fact I had yet to take the three achievement tests that were required for admission to Brown?

None of it made any difference.

Even though the acceptance came with an asterisk.

"Even though you've already graduated from high school, you still have to graduate from Worcester," Stan Ward, the Brown coach, wrote me.

I barely read it. It was only April, spring starting to creep into New England on little cat's feet, the campus coming alive in shades of green. I could see the end of the year, the prospect of another summer, my life about to return to normal. I looked at my year in prep school as a long battle I had just about won. The Beatles, some strange new group from England, had been all over the radio since February, complete with their shaggy hair that we didn't quite know what to make of. Little did any of us know then that this group would eventually change all of us in ways that were inconceivable in the winter of 1964. But life was getting better. Except for Dinah. In our long, dragged-out war of a relationship we once again were supposedly back together, although neither of us really knew what that meant anymore. We now seemed to circle each other like wary alleycats.

One Friday afternoon, with the promise of summer in the air, Mike Flaherty and I took the bus into Boston, supposedly to spend the weekend with Dinah. It was the afternoon of the Red Sox home opener, and as the bus wove its way through the towns of Framingham and Natick we listened to the game on the radio. It was the first game in Fenway Park for Tony Conigliaro, a local kid from nearby Lynn, who was starting in right field for the Red Sox. He had received a lot of attention in spring training, was considered a star of the future. He was nineteen years old and at his first time at bat in Fenway Park he hit a home run.

I had just turned nineteen a couple of days before, saw us as somehow linked together. For the next few years, even though I wasn't really a baseball fan anymore, I would always follow him in the box scores, a constant reminder of that warm spring afternoon in Boston in 1964 when we both had been nineteen together, him hitting a home run in Fenway Park, me in the process of getting dumped by my longtime girlfriend. Conigliaro would go on to have great success, the handsome kid with the home-run swing, before being beaned in the summer of 1967 in the middle of the Red Sox's "Impossible Dream" season, a night that changed his life. There would be several comebacks after that, but never again would he realize the potential of his youth, the golden promise of that afternoon when he homered in his first at-bat in Fenway, everything ahead of him. He died young, dropping dead of a heart attack at forty-five.

Flaherty and I ended up drinking beer in a Back Bay apartment that afternoon before we went over and picked up Dinah and a couple of her friends to go to a party on Beacon Hill. It was twilight, and I was already drunk when Dinah got into the car next to me. Gerry and the Pacemakers, another of the new British groups, were on the radio. They were singing about a *"ferry across the Mersey"* and time passing. I wished we were back home instead of driving down Beacon Street toward some party and our own uncertain future together.

The party was upstairs on Myrtle Street, the underbelly of Beacon Hill, full of rooming houses and run-down apartments. It was a warm night, a crowded apartment, the party spilling down the stairs and out onto the front steps as kids passed around bottles of wine and made Boston Strangler jokes. The Strangler had been terrorizing the city for about a year now, his presence hovering over Boston like a menacing thunderhead.

Dinah avoided me. Or so I thought. We no longer seemed able to talk to each other, as though the arguing was all we had left, skewered emotions that had twisted and scarred. She went into another room, I continued to drink. With each beer I got more angry. I was fed up with Dinah and her jerking around my emotions, told myself that I didn't need her anymore.

A while later I saw her dancing with some guy who looked liked he was doing a Tab Hunter impression. He never saw my punch. It caught him high on his forehead, toppling him over. I jumped on him, trying to punch his blond face, obliterate it, before someone grabbed my arm and broke it all up. Dinah looked at me as though she had never seen me before.

"What are you doing?" she asked, her eyes rimmed with tears.

I didn't know. I couldn't remember the last fight I'd been in. It was all so out-of-character, fueled by jealousy and too many beers and god knows what other demons that seeing Dinah dance with someone else had unleashed.

"Come on," I said, maneuvering her through the crowd and down the stairs. "We're going to settle a few things. Right now."

"There's nothing to settle," she said. "It's over and that's it. We have nothing in common anymore. Why can't you just accept that? Why can't you just accept it's over? Why can't we just be friends? Why does it have to end like this?"

It went on like this for a while, verbal barrages tossed back and forth like grenades; I was getting more frustrated, she getting more distant, before she finally said, "That's it. I'm going back to the dorm. Please don't call me anymore."

Soon after she left two police cars came, their lights flashing, four cops out in the narrow street.

"Why don't you go catch your fucking strangler?" someone yelled. "Go catch your fucking strangler and leave us alone."

Off in the distance a siren wailed. It all seemed a long way from Barrington.

The morning of graduation was sunny and warm, the promise of summer. I awoke feeling nauseous. My parents were coming for the ceremony thinking everything had gone according to plan. I hadn't told them about Stan Ward's letter, about how I had to graduate from Worcester Academy to get into Brown. Hadn't told them that my academic situation was precarious, for the simple reason that I had hoped I'd get lucky, like all those times when you throw up a bad shot but get a lucky bounce and the ball drops in anyway. But now graduation was only a few hours away.

There was a meeting that morning for several of us who were in danger of not graduating. We sat in the basement of Kingsley Hall waiting to have an individual conference with a kindly man with a soft crinkly face whom everyone called Dutch.

"You are in a unique situation," he said. "You have been accepted to Brown, one of the finest academic schools in the country, and you can't get out of here."

He stopped, the silence hanging in the air between us. I said nothing. What was there to say?

"Oh well," he continued. "Whether you're going to be able to stay in Brown is another issue. But that's your problem."

He pushed a piece of paper across the desk in front of me.

"This is your transcript," he said, pointing to the courses. The fourth one on the list said, "Review Mathematics," not

the Introduction to Trigonometry I had taken and had so glo-
riously failed. The grade read 60.

"This is just between us," he said with a conspiratorial
wink. "Congratulations on graduating."

I shook his hand and, as the relief washed over me, got up
to walk away.

"Good luck," he said. "I think you're going to need it."

Who needed luck?

I had my jump shot, and it hadn't let me down yet.

5

In front of Brown University, at the top of College Street, which runs from downtown Providence up a steep hill to the campus, are two black, wrought-iron gates. Campus legend has it that they only open twice in a Brown undergraduate's life: the first day, and graduation morning. That I arrived late on the first day of freshman week, the gates already having closed for the day, should have been an omen.

It was the fall of 1964, and though the Beatles already had exploded into the American consciousness everyone at Brown still wanted to look like a Beach Boy. Either that, or some Tab Hunter clone. The campus was a sea of chino pants and Shetland sweaters, of loafers and short hair. Vietnam was just some faraway place that showed up on the news every once in a while, something that had nothing to do with us.

I spent the afternoon sprawled on Raffa's couch in Barrington watching a pro football game on television, and by the time I'd gotten to the dorm, the afternoon shadows had lengthened. On all the narrow streets that surrounded the campus cars were being unpacked; the dorms were full of eager students and the promise of new beginnings. Unfortunately, it all seemed a bit anticlimactic to me. I already had been away to school, already had my new beginnings. Or so I thought. To me, this was coming home, and I approached it as though I were some grizzled combat veteran whose fate it was to be stuck in a barracks with a flock of new recruits.

The night before several of us had been hanging around the parking lot in the Newport Creamery in Barrington, one of the unofficial hangouts. We sat on cars, silhouetted by a luminous September moon. It had been one of those nights when the feeling of change was in the air. So many kids were already off to school. There was nothing to do. Dinah was gone, our relationship finally over. Barrington seemed small, used up, a place that now belonged exclusively in the past tense.

Raffa and I sat on the hood of his white American Rambler, the one where he pushed a lever and the seats fell down. He already had left college in Worcester and was now back home at Barrington College, a small Christian school in the north end of town, planning to live at home and play basketball. In front of us was Steve Harlow, who had flunked out of a small college in New Hampshire, now was back in Barrington where he and one of his ex–football buddies liked to ride around town naked, periodically stopping to ask people for directions. The year before he had written me a letter from college saying he really liked it because he played cards all day and was making so much money that he could almost pay for his tuition. The only problem was he spelled it *too-wishin.*

"Fuckin' Brown," he said, shaking his head. "I don't believe it. Fuckin' Ivy League."

"Don't worry," I said. "I'll probably flunk out by Thanksgiving."

"So what," Harlow said. "You can always say you went to
Brown. You can say it for the rest of your life. It'll be a great
routine."

So I went to Brown with a mixture of academic trepidation,
and right away my fears were confirmed. English Composi-
tion was held at eight in the morning, taught by a graduate
student in black horn-rimmed glasses and tweedy sports jackets that were a couple of sizes too big. My papers came back
bleeding, covered with red marks. I knew nothing about
metaphors, symbolism, building a rhetorical argument. I really
knew nothing about anything. I looked around at my classmates, who all seemed so much more academically advanced
than I was, and wondered what I had been doing all those
years in high school. Why did I have no idea what these things
were? Had I simply been in the wrong classes? Had I been
even awake?

French was even worse. It, too, was taught by a graduate
student, a woman who actually conducted the class in French.
Although I already had had three years of French, I certainly
couldn't speak it. I thought of French class in high school and
saw images of lost hours in the language lab, earphones on,
speaking words that made no sense to me, all the while hoping the teacher wasn't listening.

"Whew," said one kid after one of the first classes. "I'm
going to have to put in a couple of all-nighters just to catch
up."

All-nighters? Was he serious? I knew I wasn't going to stay
up all night to study French. I also knew there was no way I

could ever pass this course. So I just stopped going. A week went by. Then another. Still another. Eventually, I couldn't go, for too much time had passed.

I had arrived at Brown with all sorts of academic intentions, intentions that went up in smoke as soon as the leaves began to turn. I already had drifted into bad habits of missing too many classes, lacking both the discipline to organize my day and the dedication to realize that if I wasn't diligent the semester was going to unravel before me like some old carpet left out in the rain. Unlike my roommate, who never missed a class and made a list every night of the things he would try to accomplish the next day—writing papers in September that weren't due until November—I spent the first few months of college as if it were summer camp. Too many mornings I slunk back under the covers, back into some dreamy world where there were no metaphors and no papers that came back bleeding, only the comfortable warmth of my own inertia. Too many nights I avoided my desk as if some virus were in the drawers, watching the big hit TV shows *Laugh-In* and *Hullabaloo* instead.

Many nights Harlow would come visit. Bored back in Barrington, he loved to come hang out in my room, entertaining the kids on my floor as if he were some booth in a carnival. He talked of cockfights and shooting cats and other activities that seemed a long way from the Ivy League, and often punctuated his stories by periodically slamming his forehead into the wall, telling everyone that the forehead was the hardest part of the body. Everyone on my floor loved Harlow. He seemed to represent some free spirit exempt from studying and preparing for classes and the inherent expectations that went with being a freshman at Brown.

The implication was that I had joined him in these activi-

ties, which, combined with my all-too-obvious disregard for
my classes, gave me a certain panache in the insular world of
the dorm. I was the cocky, self-assured guy who didn't seem
to care about anything. And if I knew it was more complicated
than that, knew that my supposed academic indifference was
merely a shield to hide a profound sense of academic inferi-
ority, I liked the image.

So the fall became a series of lost days that eventually ran
together. Invariably sleeping too late. Getting up feeling guilty
for missing too many classes, then wandering out to the gym
in the early afternoon, then either going out drinking or
watching TV in the dorm lounge, falling farther and farther
behind, totally immersed in the present tense, not wanting to
think about the academic guillotine that was getting sharper
and sharper over my head. By the time the leaves began to fall
in November I was already too far gone in English and
French, holding onto C's in Sociology and Classics, only because they were introductory courses held in large lecture halls
where if you didn't pull down your pants and urinate in the
class the worst you could get was the so-called "gentleman
C," which seemed to be as much a part of Brown then as
"mixers" with neighboring women's colleges and Saturday-
night parties.

I didn't go to French class again until December, when,
lured by some sense of pervading guilt, I finally went back to
class. The teacher, dark-haired and earnest, looked at me in
disbelief.

"Look," she said afterward. "This is my first year teaching
and I don't want to flunk anybody. Do anything on the final
and I will pass you, if you promise me you won't take any
more French. You can do it. The final is not going to be difficult. It's going to be all translation and if you just brush up on

your vocabulary I know you can do well enough to pass."

She told me to make vocabulary cards, French on one side, English on the other. So I went away determined to study, determined to pass, giving myself a pep talk as I walked across the campus green. But it didn't last long. A couple of weeks later, convinced that my flash cards were a charade, I threw them out my third-floor window, one after another, watching them flutter into the breeze and float down to Thayer Street, my academic hopes floating down with them.

Brown's Marvel Gymnasium, a redbrick monument to a lost era, was almost two miles away from the campus. It had been built in 1927, then considered a showcase of sorts, part of a complex that included the football stadium across Elmgrove Avenue and numerous athletic fields nearby. But by 1964 its glory days were as gone as the big-band era. It had hissing pipes, rafters in the ceiling, a skylight, and lockers in the basement. There also was the catwalk that went up to the top of the building and a running track that circled the court, reminiscent of every YMCA and Boys' Club, complete with people hanging over the railings. It was a college gym, nothing more, a musty old place where you could almost smell the memories and hear the echoes of yesterday's cheers.

It was located deep in the heart of Providence's residential East Side, an athletic outpost in the middle of a predominantly Jewish neighborhood, removed from the campus geographically as well as spiritually. In a sense, intercollegiate athletics was the university's bastard child. Football was in near despair, losing season tacked onto losing season until they all seemed indistinguishable, the alumni embarrassed, the students disinterested.

Basketball was even worse, although I didn't realize that at the time I was being recruited.

What I didn't know was that one player had quit after announcing he "wasn't into sweating anymore." One had gone off to Sweden for a semester and had never come back. Another had quit to become a surfer. One reserve always went to the wrong lane in layup drills, doing his best to screw up every practice drill, calling himself a basketball version of a guerrilla fighter. The trainer once refused to tape a player before a game, saying, "Hey, you're not going to play anyway." He also routinely bet against us with one of Providence's innumerable bookies, and was incensed in the locker room one night after a big upset, screaming, "How could you guys win? You guys suck."

Stan Ward had been the coach for ten years. He also was the baseball coach, and at various times in his tenure at Brown had been the freshman football coach and the golf coach, too. Summers he worked at a camp in the Poconos—didn't own a camp like the coaches of today do—worked at one.

He never had had the luxury of being a full-time basketball coach even in a league that included Princeton's Bill Bradley, then the best college player in America, and a couple of teams among the best in the country. He had no full-time assistant coach, no one to help him recruit. Back then it was only Stan, all by himself. And by the mid-1960s it had started to get to him. There had been too many late-night bus rides home from losing games, too many battles with the admissions office over kids they wouldn't take, too many games he went into knowing the other coach had too many of the best players. Too many practices where the track team was running on the track overhead and some guy was kicking a soccer ball in the corner; too many nights realizing that it wasn't ever to happen for him at Brown, couldn't happen for him, not in the way he once had hoped.

But if Stan seemed beaten down, we had the best freshman team in years.

The other guard was Rick Landau, a five-foot-nine sparkplug with dark hair and thick thighs from the eastern Pennsylvania coal country. He was hardworking, dedicated, an excellent student, someone who seemed at eighteen to have his life already mapped out. He reminded me a lot of Jay Sarles, and he quickly became our unofficial leader, although on a team with so many eccentric personalities being a leader was virtually impossible.

The center was Steve Sigur, six foot seven, blond, from Atlanta. He spoke with a decided drawl, was good-natured as a puppy, and liked to play pickup games in bare feet. He was a strange mixture of intellectual and hayseed. His entire demeanor spoke of the Old South, yet he was purported to be some physics prodigy, and read things like James Joyce's *Ulysses* for fun. One forward was Rod Gillmore, six foot six, from upstate New York somewhere. He had a picture of his hometown sweetheart on his bureau, seemed to miss as many classes as I did, and wandered around the campus looking forlorn, only rising out of his lethargy every afternoon to go to the gym.

The other was Greg Donaldson, and no one knew what to make of him. He was six-four, looked like a leaner, more athletic version of Elliott Gould, and considered the greatest impediment to his basketball life the fact that he had not been born black. He was from Long Island where his father supposedly once had been a Communist, his older brother one of the first people on Long Island who refused to salute the flag in school. Donaldson always wore desert boots, tight dungarees, and faded surfing T-shirts, and paraded around the campus like a migrant worker. He seemingly never studied, but got good grades anyway, and invariably would say things like, "Coca-Cola and United Fruit run the world"—statements that seemed so daffy to me in that fall of 1964 that I didn't even try to rebut them.

He also divided the world into two categories: "studly" and "flitly." "Studly" was skintight Levi's, Negroes, Clint Eastwood in *The Good, the Bad, and the Ugly*, playing pool, sleeping until noon, low white Converse sneakers, dunking a basketball, Hobie surfboards, Navy CPO jackets, Hemingway heroes, and looking cool and unaffected at all times. Most of all, he said, "studly" was having character.

"Flitly" was studying all the time, walking around campus carrying a green bookbag, worrying about grades, wearing Hush Puppies, sucking up to teachers, and taking anything seriously.

There were others on the freshmen team, including one who threw up left-handed corkscrew jump shots who, for some unknown reason, was called "Vector." One blond kid called everything good "Fat City," although none of us ever knew why.

All of us had been very good high-school players, stars of our respective teams. Now we'd all been thrown together, sink or swim, grappling for some new identity, something to make us unique. This was happening all over campus, kids who only the year before had been the best and the brightest of their high-school class, and had played off it, used it, were now quickly realizing they needed some new identity. So we had the kid in the dorm who stayed in his walk-in closet virtually all day watching soap operas. Others who got so drunk on weekends they would wake up the next morning in their own vomit. Still another who was called "Road-Show Howie," for his propensity every weekend to go off to some women's college where he'd invariably perform a succession of social atrocities, only to come back and brag about them. There also were a few who walked around campus, clothes tattered, as if on their way to meet Bob Dylan at the espresso bar on Thayer Street. Brown was new territory; we were all homesteaders looking for a place to settle, trying on new identities as if they were new shirts, seeing which ones fit.

In a sense I was exempt. I knew what my identity was. It was the same as it always had been: I was a basketball player.

And from those first few days in the gym, when we all got together and played pickup games, I sensed I was somehow different. Although we'd all been recruited to play basketball, were all at Brown for essentially the same reason, I felt as if the game were somehow more important to me. Landau had his academics, Sigur his physics, Donaldson his convictions. Only Gillmore seemed as lost away from Marvel Gym as I did. Without basketball I not only knew I wouldn't have been there, I also knew I wouldn't have wanted to be there.

As soon as the season started we were winning and I was scoring points, all of this recorded in the sports section of the Providence *Journal,* which was read back in Barrington. No matter that I already was well on my way to becoming an academic disaster. All anyone knew back home was that I was playing well. In their eyes I already was a big success at Brown. Not only was I the only person from Barrington playing major college basketball, I was the only player from my old high-school league, only one of a small handful from Rhode Island.

The freshman games were played before the varsity games, usually in front of only a smattering of people. It was very different from high school, basketball without the fizz. Only two nights that year were like it had been in high school, the gym packed, an electricity in the air that almost ignited. One was when Providence College came across town to play, a night when Marvel Gym was packed for the freshman game too. The other was when Princeton and Bill Bradley came to Providence. Bradley was arguably the best college player in the country, certainly the most famous. His Princeton team that year eventually would go all the way to the Final Four, almost unheard-of for an Ivy League school.

Bradley was a presence in our lives in a way he never could have understood. We talked about him endlessly, dissected his game, tried to copy some of his moves. By choosing to play in the Ivy League he validated the league, gave it a basketball importance it never had known before. Bradley had the kind of fame that transcended being an All-American; he was an almost mythical figure, the embodiment of the student-athlete, the great player, the potential Rhodes Scholar. His legend would soon spread in a famous *New Yorker* article by the noted writer John McPhee, the article which later grew into the book *A Sense of Where You Are*.

The key scene was when the two of them were standing near a basket at Princeton. While talking, Bradley took a shot without looking, which went in. McPhee couldn't believe it.

"How did you do that without looking?" he asked.

"It's no big deal," Bradley countered. "You just have to have a sense of where you are."

Greg Donaldson loved to trash him. He called him an ugly player, overrated, an efficient robot, an argument that seemed almost sacrilegious to the rest of us. To Donaldson, the only players he truly respected were black ones, the "studly" ones, like Jimmy Walker, then a sophomore at Providence College. Walker was one of the best sophomores in the country, one of the first generation of black players who were starting to change the college game. He often dribbled through his legs, which none of us had ever seen before, and spun around with the ball, also something not in any of the basketball text-books. Walker had all kinds of playground moves.

He was a sneak preview of basketball's future, as if already there were two ways to play basketball, two different ways that would become more pronounced in the following decades: the white, fundamental textbook game, and the improvisa-tional, black game that had grown up amidst the crumbling asphalt and shattered dreams of the inner cities, basketball as the city game. That was a tradition we all were aware of, es-pecially the kids who came from New York. They were for-ever telling stories of New York City playground legends, guys like Jackie Jackson who could take quarters off the top of the backboard even though he was only six foot five, and six-two Earl Manigault who supposedly could dunk two balls at the same time.

I loved these stories. They reminded me of basketball camp, of being part of the game's subculture, a giant network that I was a part of.

Donaldson loved Walker's game. It supported his adage that "a studly shot missed was better than a feeble shot swished." He lived for those rare moments when he dunked. He loved to take whirling drives to the hoop, magnificent solo flights where the trip seemed more important than the result. His jump shot seemed to resemble some piece of art nouveau, all wasted motion and excess. No matter that his jumper rarely went in. It was the style he was in love with.

It was, of course, a philosophy that clashed with Stan Ward's, a basketball purist, a teacher in the best sense of the term. He looked at Donaldson and saw potential thwarted by fantasies. Stan was forever taking Donaldson aside and

giving him fatherly talks on how he needed to mature as a
player, a euphemism for stopping all the foolishness and start
playing the game the right way, the textbook way. One particular day he had spent almost a half hour before practice
talking to Donaldson on these same themes, Donaldson nod-
ding at all the appropriate times, so surely Stan must have
thought that he was finally getting through to this new freshman. A couple of hours later, there was Stan walking out of
practice when he saw Donaldson dribble at breakneck speed
down the court, try some outrageous move, only to trip and
fall on his face. Stan just shook his head and walked slowly to
the door that led downstairs, as if the weight of the basketball
world and its changing realities was lodged squarely between
his shoulders.

We only lost three games that year as freshmen, and Stan
was looking forward to the following year. I led the team in
scoring, had two games over thirty, and Stan was forever
telling me that I had to do better in school, fearful that if I had
another semester as disastrous as the first, I would flunk out.
He even met me and Gillmore one day in the cafeteria in an
attempt to teach us how to study.

"You have to organize your class notes every night," he
told us.

"What do you do if you don't go to class?" Gillmore whispered to me afterward. Our version of a Zen question.

I didn't play another game until February of the following
year.

On academic probation, I spent the first semester of my
sophomore year being allowed to practice with the team, but
not play in any games. The week after Christmas the team
went to a tournament in Rochester. I stayed home. On the
two nights they played I rode around Barrington trying to

find a spot where I could hear the game through the static on the radio, spots that kept changing.

It was the first time basketball had ever been taken away from me, and it made me want it more than ever. I needed to get at least a 2.0 grade point average, which was the equivalent of getting four C's and it was the motivation I needed to do better in school. I got up every morning. I went to class. I did homework.

It was a motivation directly tied to basketball. I was never a college student who just happened to play basketball; I was a basketball player who had to pass enough courses to stay eligible. I measured courses by how easy they were, not how good. They were something to get through, obstacle courses that had to be maneuvered by any means possible, whether by plagiarizing term papers, or using *Cliff Notes* instead of reading the actual books. I didn't know any of my teachers, never talked to them, was intimidated by them. I saw them as adversaries, people with the power to take something away from me that was so terribly important, certainly not people with my best interests at stake. They weren't there to help me; they were just another opponent.

So when I was finally eligible I felt reborn.

I was joining a team in the bottom half of the Ivy League, waist-deep in mediocrity. We were a mixture of upperclassmen and sophomores. Donaldson had started all year and Landau and Sigur had been two of the first reserves into the game. Gillmore was gone, having transferred to Hofstra, his absence a powerful reminder to me that Brown was concerned with a lot more than jump shots.

On the second weekend I was eligible we took a bus for our annual trek to Princeton and Pennsylvania, Ivy League games always being played on Friday and Saturday nights. It was

early February, and to the upperclassmen these trips had become nuisances, long rides to play games we had little chance
of winning, followed by long rides back to Providence after
the Saturday-night games, invariably arriving back on campus
in the wee hours of the morning tired and defeated, a long way
from the supposed glamour of college sports. To me, though,
the trip was the equivalent of a victory parade past cheering
throngs. Driving through New York City, Yankee Stadium
out the window. The glistening spires of Manhattan, with all
their promise. I saw this all as a tangible symbol that I had
truly made it as a basketball player. This wasn't taking the
schoolbus in high school to Warren and Bristol. This was stay-
ing in hotels and eating in restaurants. This was the big-time,
and I savored all of it.

"Do you know what kind of defense Princeton plays?" said
a kid in the back of the bus, as the bus crossed the George
Washington Bridge. "Jungle D."

A jungle noise came from the other side of the bus, the
piercing sound of a crow. Then the sound of a monkey. Another shriek. The bus was a cacaphony of yells, shrieks that
lasted for a couple of minutes. Up in the front of the bus was
Stan Ward. He never turned around.

What was he thinking? That boys will be boys? What did
it feel like to be the coach of a losing Ivy League team, and to
play in an old antiquated gym two miles from campus? Every
year to go out and recruit more players, all the while knowing that you could never recruit enough good ones to really
make a difference. And now to sit on a bus stuck in New York
City traffic on the start of a weekend that only promised two
more defeats in a season that had seen too many of them already, and listen to your team act like some fifth-grade class
on a field trip to Plymouth Rock.

If inappropriate, the noises were telling. Princeton did indeed play "Jungle D," a clamping, oppressive man-to-man game that had us completely out of our offense very quickly. Even if Bradley had graduated, the Tigers were still very good. They were coached by Butch van breda Kolff, who later would go on to coach the Los Angeles Lakers and become one of the true Damon Runyon characters of basketball, and they were appreciably better than we were. At the half we were already down by about twenty. I had played only briefly.

In the second half, though, with about ten minutes to play, I got into the game. I quickly made a shot from deep in the left corner. Then another from out behind the circle. Then another. By now the guy guarding me was no longer thinking about the score of the game. He was embarrassed, his face clenched. I got the ball again and he was all over me. It didn't matter. I was off in some private place again, just me and the ball, just like all those times in the backyard as a kid, like it had been against Warren my junior year in high school, off in the zone somewhere.

"Shoot. . . . Shoot!" the crowd yelled, every time I got the ball, regardless of where I was on the floor. I had become the diversion, a little pocket of excitement in a game that essentially was over in the first half. So I kept shooting and the ball kept going in. I ended up with seventeen points.

Back on the bus going to Philadelphia to play Penn the next night, listening to some radio station that talked about the Delaware Valley, about to stay in a hotel, it felt like living right in the middle of a fantasy.

Again, my shooting skill had come through for me, set me apart. Once again basketball had distinguished me. Once again I was playing, and all was well with the world.

• • •

It would stay that way all through the next year, through a December trip to Georgia and Florida, the first time I ever had been in an airplane; through a year that saw me average seventeen points a game, a year that fulfilled my adolescent dreams of being a college basketball player. My name was in the paper. Games against Providence College and the University of Rhode Island were on the radio. I learned to cling to my rather meager success as if it were a lifeline. But once again, we were a mediocre team at best, Donaldson missing the entire year with a dislocated shoulder from a surfing accident, our inside game not good enough to be anything more than a second division Ivy team.

For playing basketball at Brown was never easy.

Unlike high school, it was possible to walk the campus in virtual anonymity. There were no perks that came with being a player, no outward rewards. Even getting to the gym was difficult, standing on Thayer Street in the cold waiting for the bus to come. Every year there were a new batch of freshman players, eager and wide-eyed, all arriving with their own hopes and basketball dreams. They would play on the freshman team. Then you would see most of them start to drop by the wayside, worn down by it all, eventually make their own separate peace with the game, move on to other things. Brown was full of failed athletes, kids who had played in high school and now had met their level of incompetence, an athletic version of the Peter Principle before anyone ever heard of the term.

Sometimes, at fleeting moments, I envied these kids who had put sports behind them. At such times I tried to envision a life without basketball. I pictured myself going off to the library in the afternoons, going out drinking at night, going off to girls' colleges on weekends. But these moments came and went in a puff of smoke, and there would be another day, another practice, and my life would go on, a treadmill that took me to the next game.

But it was never easy. So we learned to take our rewards in smaller packages. A win here. A good game there. Little victories measured out in coffee spoons.

Our best player that year was Alan Fishman, a senior guard from Brooklyn, left-handed and crafty, someone who later would rise to the virtual top of Chemical Bank. He had played in high school at Erasmus Hall, on the same team with Billy Cunningham, the great North Carolina All-American who later starred in the NBA, and "the Fish" suffered neither fools nor bad players gladly.

"Look at him," he said to me during the middle of the game at Princeton as we were getting drilled, pointing to one of our reserves who was in the game and playing badly. "We're playing Princeton and he's in the game. What the fuck."

He was particularly tough on a couple of sophomores who were from the South. They looked at the Fish and his New York swagger as if he were from some far-off planet. To them, the Fish was a source of mystery, always seeming to be off somewhere in a hurry, as if he had some secret life. Like the day he was excused from practice for some unexplained reason.

"Where's Fish?" asked a sophomore named Bob Buck, all wide-eyed, the Georgia backwoods in his speech.

"The Fish is not like the rest of us," Donaldson said. "He's a busy man. He's got all sorts of interests he had to attend to. Today he's in New York."

"New York?" asked Buck, perplexed, full of wide-eyed wonder. "What's he doing in New York?"

"Did you ever hear of 'Fish Sticks'?" Donaldson asked.

But we had our moments, splashes of color against the dull canvas of mediocrity. The highlight was against Princeton in Marvel Gym. Bill Bradley had graduated two years earlier, but Princeton was still a great team, and came to Providence with an 18–1 record and ranked fourth in the country.

They had played at Yale the night before, had won a squeaker. They also had a *Sports Illustrated* writer traveling with them. He was all set to do a cover story that would appear the next week, one that featured guard Gary Walters and center Chris Thomforde on the cover. The gist of that story would be how Princeton, now two years removed from Bill Bradley, was still one of the elite teams in the country, a rare feat for an Ivy League team.

Marvel was packed, the old gym electric. Earlier in the year they had crushed us, and they were supposed to do it again. They had a front line made up of the six-foot-ten Thomforde, and two six-foot-eight players, John Haarlow and Ed Hummer, who later played in the NBA. There was no way we could match up with them physically, but we were playing a match-up zone that was giving them problems. At the half we were only training by five, and we came flying into the locker room, all but bouncing off the walls.

"Calm down," said Stan Ward when he entered the room.

Stan was rarely emotional in the locker room. Just the opposite. He didn't want his teams being too high. Instead, he wanted us to be cerebral, especially defensively. He forever was trying to calm us down. The few exceptions were when he lost his temper, which wasn't often. Once, though, continually watching Sigur wipe his blond hair out of his eyes, he grabbed a pair of scissors, went over to Sigur, grabbed a handful of hair and clipped it off.

"Take good shots," Stan said. "Keep controlling the tempo. The pressure is all on them. We can win if we play smart."

We hardly heard him. We were in the game with the number-four team in the country in a packed Marvel Gym. Four minutes into the half we were leading by five and the building was in an incredible din.

I had had a great game, hitting tough shots in the second half that kept us in the game, the crowd in an uproar, smelling the upset. It was another one of nights when time seemed suspended, slowed down somehow, the basket looking big and seductive. The lead seesawed back and fourth after that, but after I hit a bomb from the right corner with 1:58 to play, we were up 54–53.

With a little over a minute to play I stole a pass, the biggest defensive play of my life. The crowd exploded with a deafening roar of noise. We were leading by one, we had the ball, were poised for one of the biggest upsets of the college basketball season, the kind of win that redeems a season, maybe even gets some good ink in *Sports Illustrated*. There was no "shot clock" in college basketball then, so we had the floor spread, were essentially killing the clock, for Princeton didn't want to foul.

The rule is simple in this situation. No shots except a layup. Make them have to foul. Make them make the mistake.

Our senior forward was Dave Gale, skinny and six foot seven, who had a good first step to the basket. In practice he was always beating someone off the dribble and taking one big step across the lane for the jam. It was his signature move, the best thing he did. Now he was ready to do it again. I had the ball on the left side, under pressure. Gale came out of the corner for the pass, then reversed direction, going back-door. I threw him the pass of my life, a hard bounce pass which he easily caught, took one dribble, and started the move to the open basket we all had seen so many times before in practice. Only, for some inexplicable reason, he stopped about four feet from the basket and threw up an off-balance shot. It rolled around the rim and slid off.

Thomforde got the rebound, Gale fouled him. Thomforde made the two throws giving Princeton the lead, 55–54.

We came back and held the ball, called timeout with eighteen seconds left. The play was for the left-handed Fishman to come off a high screen and try to take the ball to the basket. I was to be in the left corner, and as Fishman turned the corner and headed to the basket, the defense reacting to him, he had the option to either take the ball to the basket or throw it to me in the corner.

But Princeton went into a zone, and we never picked it up. Fishman came off the screen, but there was someone right there in front of him. He lost the ball, as I stood virtually alone in the corner.

We lost by one.

The last game of the season was Jimmy Walker's last game in Providence, which had incredible significance at the time. He had been the best player in the school's history, complete with a palpable charisma, the sense he was a man playing against boys. He was leading the country in scoring. In a few months he would be the first pick in the '67 NBA draft. The crowd was all but shoehorned into Marvel Gym as both teams were on the floor warming up. Only problem was, no Walker. He finally walked into the gym five minutes before the game in a fur hat, regal as a young prince come to meet his subjects.

The game was nip-and-tuck, our zone defense slowing Walker down, keeping us in the game. But with a couple of minutes left and Providence leading by a few, we had to come out of our zone and start playing man-to-man, with me matched up against Walker. It was an assignment that filled me with dread.

Walker was almost impossible to play man-to-man. The year before, he had scored fifty points in Madison Square Garden, and two guys from Boston College had fallen down trying to guard him. On that night a teenage black kid had sat in the first row of the balcony. Every time Walker would score, always by using a succession of spin moves and jukes that would free him for a soft fifteen-footer, the kid would get up from his seat, walk several rows up the aisle, slap palms with another black kid, then return to his seat. Over and over he did this, never saying a word.

Near the end of that game, Providence safely ahead, Walker was taken out. He sat on the bench with his arm up over his shoulder, palm up, as a group of kids lined up behind him in a procession, each kid slapping his palm. Walker never turned around.

Donaldson said it was one of the studliest things he'd ever seen.

Now I had to guard Walker, and I had never been particularly good defensively. I also had four fouls, one short of disqualification.

He came down the court with the ball, his body going all different ways, as I waited. He quickly turned his back, as he usually did. *Stay on your feet,* I told myself. *Fall down and you'll be embarrassed forever.*

Walker started his routine, spinning back and forth with the ball, and I was powerless to do anything about it. He faked left, then quickly came back right, started to rock, and I felt myself lose my balance. So I pushed him. Pushed him even

though I knew it was a foul. Pushed him because I knew it was
better to foul out than fall down.

When the referee's whistle blew, I turned and started walking toward the bench. My junior year was over.

"What kind of a horseshit foul was that?" Stan Ward said
disgustedly, as I walked by him to the bench.

You guard him, I wanted to say.

But I moved through that season as if in a period of grace,
loving all of it. The games. The trips. The practices. As though
I was fulfilling a personal destiny that had started out there in
the driveway in the dark, dreaming my penny-arcade dreams.

My teammates had the game in perspective, were at Brown
to prepare for some defined future, even if the Vietnam War
cast a lengthening shadow over everything. Still, there was
the sense among them that that they were at Brown as a part
of some articulated vision of the future, one that wasn't going
to include basketball. They seemed to have the ability to make
a separate peace with the game.

For me, it was still much like it had been in high school. I
lived from game to game, from season to season, without any
vision that extended beyond college, no tangible goals that
went beyond playing my last game. School was something to
get through in order to stay eligible, a necessary end, just like
it always had been. The game filled my life, gave it its focus.
Where my teammates had so obviously evolved, were using
college as a means of moving from adolescence to adulthood,
basketball was still the way I defined myself, my compass in
a world of unexplored roads.

That spring I was in a course called The Philosophy of Literature. Or maybe it was The Literature of Philosophy. To
this day I'm not sure.

It was a typical course for me at the time, supposed to be

easy, no required attendance, a large lecture hall where no one knew if you were there or not. I had become better at school by now, not by being a better student, but by being craftier about it. The right courses. Cramming for finals. Adhering to Donaldson's "Theory of No Superfluous Knowledge."

"If the test is an hour long you, only want to know an hour's worth of knowledge," he said. "That way you don't have to worry about what the question is. Or what is relevant and what's not. Just write everything you know."

Yet nothing had really changed.

Since this particular course had started in early February, in the heart of the season, I had rarely gone. Certainly I hadn't read any of the books.

On the day before the midsemester I went to a class that was supposed to be a review for the test, taking notes furiously, trying to make up half a semester's work in an hour. That night there was a study session, a half a dozen guys, another chance to play catch-up.

So I listened to all the talk of all the books, until one guy said, "I guess that does it. It should be no sweat."

"Wait," I said, going through my notebook. "There's one more. It's right here in my notes. It's the last book he mentioned. Right here. *Doctor Zay-goon.*"

There was a silence.

"Yeah, that's it," I said, trying to decipher my notes. "*Doctor Zay-goon.* Or something like that."

More silence.

"You don't mean *Darkness at Noon,* do you?" someone asked.

But at least now I knew what periodicals were.

All around me were the signs of change. The summer of '67

was changing America, with riots in many American cities, including the big ones in Detroit and Newark, pictures of flames of fire licking the sky, America coming apart. The war continued to grow, complete with growing opposition to it.

And in June the culture changed. The Monterey Pop Festival launched the careers of Janis Joplin and Jimi Hendrix, two musicians who came out of nowhere to become pop icons, though both would be dead of drug overdoses in three years. The Jefferson Airplane released an album that contained the songs "White Rabbit" and "Somebody to Love," two songs that became virtual themes for a generation. The Doors, a group named after Aldous Huxley's book about the benefits of taking psychedelic drugs, came out with "Light My Fire," the soundtrack to the summer. And the Beatles' *Sgt. Pepper* explored drug references and lyrics about "marmalade skies" and "tangerine trees." The Beatles as hippies. It was the album that legitimized the counterculture, the world's most famous group embarking on a surreal new trip, and about to take America's youth with them.

It was the summer that Negroes started to be called "blacks," spurred on by young radicals like Stokely Carmichael and H. Rap Brown. The summer where it seemed that the country was having a nervous breakdown. The summer of the Haight-Ashbury in San Francisco, a sneak preview of the future.

I missed all of it.

I was getting ready for my last college season. Every afternoon I would go to the outdoor court across the street from Barrington High School and shoot around by myself for a couple of hours. I had to make five shots in a row from several spots on the court before I could leave, my personal obstacle course. It was my way of being disciplined, and I liked the fact I was the only one there, a reaffirmation that the game meant more to me than it did to anyone else, and that shooting by myself on humid afternoons proved that. Then I had to make ten free throws in a row. Shooting a basketball by myself was still the place I felt completely comfortable, just me and the ball, over and over, a private world where no one was allowed to enter, as familiar as childhood, timeless.

Then it was off to the barbershop on County Road, which was like stepping into some time capsule, a place far removed from burning cities and *Sgt. Pepper* and an America that seemed to be coming apart. The barbershop was still a sanctuary, where the biggest issue of the day was the baseball pennant race. It was run by two brothers from nearby Bristol, Nick and Lou Conti, and if they cut hair for a living, sports were their passion. Sports were the staple of the conversation, all day, every day, year after year.

It was the same with Jack.

He was twenty-nine, sat in the barbershop every day. Jack was originally from Cleveland and the Indians were his obsession, a source of endless conversation. One day, several years before, he had been on his way to Boston to finish a college career that had been interrupted by a four-year hitch in the Air Force. He stopped for a haircut, got into a sports argument, and never left. Every morning around ten, he would drive his red-and-white Corvette to the barbershop, walk into the shop in his blue blazer as if he were on the way to some cushy job in Providence, hang up the blazer, and sit there for the next five hours. He bullshitted with the customers, flirted with the young mothers, argued about sports with Nick and Lou. All day, every day. Then at three-thirty he went home to start drinking martinis and watch *Leave It to Beaver* reruns.

One day Raffa and I were helping him move into his new

apartment. He was finally going to live with his wife, whom he'd married months before, when she discovered she was pregnant.

"See how hard this bed is?" Jack said, hitting the mattress with his fist. "Good for poonin'."

"Marriage seems like fun," Raffa said later.

Words that one day would come back to haunt him.

But I loved the insular world of the barbershop. It was one more reaffirmation that sports were more than just games; they were a place you could hide in, a way in which to both perceive the world and make some sense out of it. Every afternoon I sat in the shop, arguing about the Indians, the same conversations on different days. I wanted time to stop, to live in that summer forever, complete with the promise of another season. Where other kids my age were leaving college, starting careers, moving on to new chapters, I sat in the barbershop.

That was my world that summer, and it was about as far removed from the tumult happening in the country as you could get.

Yet there were changes even I couldn't ignore. My parents were separated, in the process of being divorced, something rare in Barrington in those days. My father lived in a small apartment in Providence, one I rarely visited. It made me uncomfortable to see the pictures of my brother and sister on his dresser, visible reminders that he now lived in a different world.

I resented him for having shattered the family, yet I never articulated this to him. He never explained to me what had happened, that he'd had an affair with another woman, although we both knew I knew. That knowledge hung in the silences between us. We never tried to fill in the blanks. Instead, we hid within the parameters of sports, as we always had done. We talked of the Red Sox's great season, the upcoming college basketball season, little else. And I came to understand that summer that sports also could be used as a buffer against your true feelings, a carapace that kept you protected, a cocoon you could retreat into and block out the world with.

My brother Geoff was already in the Coast Guard, having left college after less than a year.

He was a year and a half younger, and no doubt there were times he had come to resent my basketball playing, the fact that it seemed to dominate so much of the family's focus, whether it was our parents going to my games, or just simply the talk at the dinner table. He had gone through a particularly painful adolescence of too much drinking and not doing well in school, his friends much like him. They were Barrington's rebels, full of unfocused angst that would spill out a few years later in the counterculture.

The summer before, though, we had both worked on a golf course together in North Providence. There, away from Barrington and our defined roles, we got along fine, true brothers, linked by blood and family and a shared history. Back home it was more strained.

One night, over a long holiday evening, all the tensions erupted. My father already had left the family. My mother was away. My sister was off at camp. Geoff was having a party in our house. It had been going on for three days. Sometimes there were fifty kids there, sometimes there were ten, but they always were there. They slept on the floor. They played the music too loud. They came and went. And I resented them. Now it was late, Geoff was drunk, the house was a mess, kids sprawled everywhere.

"That's it," I said. "The party's over."

"No, it's not," he said. "It's my party, not yours."

We bantered back and forth at each other, until I pushed him.

He came back at me, and I pushed him back again, this time harder, the big brother beating on the little one, one too many times. He rushed at me and I hit him with a punch, aiming for his shoulder, not his face.

Suddenly, he picked up a large kitchen knife, came back at me in a frenzied rage, before a couple of kids grabbed him.

We had never had a fight like this, not even close. I went out to the backyard, still shaking from the emotion, equal parts rage and guilt, trying to comprehend what had just happened. I knew I had pushed him too much. I had known he was drunk, and I should have realized the potential for trouble.

A few minutes later I left the house and began riding aimlessly around town. The streets were deserted, the town as quiet as a cemetery at three in the morning. I knew I couldn't go home.

Eventually I drove over to Echo Lake, hard by the eighth hole of the Rhode Island Country Club, where Raffa and I had once gone parking with Sunde and Patsie in what was beginning now to seem like some other life. I sat in the dark listening to the radio, angry at everything. Angry at myself for provoking something that could have been avoided. Angry at my brother. Most of all, angry at my father for leaving the house and destroying our family.

The next morning a cop woke me. He stared at me as I sat up in the backseat, disoriented.

"You the basketball player?" he asked.

"Yeah," I said, rubbing the sleep from my eyes.

"Well, there's no game here," he said. "So go home."

Home, I thought. But where was it anymore?

There was the hint of other changes, too, distant thunder. The war was all over the news, impossible to ignore. It was the first television war, and it came into the living room every night with all its horror and grisly images. It complicated the future, began hanging over our lives like some haze that never burned off. In a sense it was the last summer of innocence, the last magical time when it was possible to live in the way America had been in the 1950s, with the sense that everyone was playing by the same rules, even if we all were to later learn that it always had been more complicated than that.

We spent many nights in seedy bars in Warren, places that catered to underage kids from Barrington, drinking cheap drafts with grizzled old quahoggers with nicotine-stained fingers and glassy eyes. The bars were the Rainbow and the Moonlight, places where the names promised romance and the lushness of a forties movie and the reality was of some old rummy drinking shots and beers in the corner, all the while trying to get his dog drunk. Only a few years later a couple of those kids would come back from Vietnam in pine boxes, but we spent that summer suspended in time, immersed in the present tense, as though the war was off in some parallel universe, so far removed from how we were living our lives. And surely this war was going to end soon, right? You just had to get rough with those Commies, right? Hadn't this been what we'd been told in Problems of Democracy back in high school? Get tough with the Commies and they always will back down. So why wasn't this war ending?

One night there was kid in the Moonlight who had been two years ahead of me in high school. He had been all-state in football, one of those heavyset, powerful kids who had seemed to have a five-o'clock shadow in Little League. He was sitting in a back booth with a bottle of Narragansett beer in front of

him and he seemed smaller, almost shrunken; all the strength
and power I remembered had been drained out of him. His
eyes were downcast, almost vacant. Every time he brought
the Narragansett to his lips, his hand slightly shook. He had
just come back from a year in Vietnam, and when asked about
it, had only said quietly, "It was horrible. You can't even imag-
ine how bad it is."

Someone asked another question, but he simply put out his
hand and shook his head, as if to say, No more, no more.

In the fall Brown had changed dramatically from the one
we had left in the spring. Now the weekly peace vigil in the
middle of the campus every Wednesday noon had swelled con-
siderably from the fifty or so people that had been there in the
spring. Now there was some evidence of long hair, the beginnings of a countercultural presence. The big movie was *The
Graduate,* with an unknown actor named Dustin Hoffman
playing a kid who graduates from college, then returns home
in the summer without much of a clue as to what he wants to
do in the future, someone who seems to drift through his life
to a Simon and Garfunkel soundtrack, as though caught between two conflicting views of life, the sterile suburban world
of his parents and some unarticulated future that he'd caught
a glimpse of in college. The telling scene was when Hoffman,
at his parents' party, is told by one of his parents' friends that
the future is "plastics," the one word that was supposed to
sum up a staid, uptight America that was about to go up in
smoke.

I didn't get it.

We lived in an apartment behind Hope High School, a few
blocks from the campus—Donaldson, another teammate
named Bob Purvis, and my old roommate from sophomore
year whom we called "Bluto" after the character from *Popeye.*

We all had our own rooms, except for Purvis who slept on a mattress in the dining room. He was into Zen, ate nothing but rice, and rarely said anything. Bluto was blond, blue-eyed, and powerful, could have stepped out of a poster for the Hitler Youth. He referred to himself as "the Golden Prince," constantly walked around the apartment with just a towel around his waist, and never walked by a mirror without stopping to stare lovingly at himself and watch his arm muscles flex. He flirted with the idea of going off to be a fighter pilot, talked of one day going to Vietnam "to kill gooks," and to verbally harangued the people at the peace vigils, calling them "flits" and "peace creeps."

Donaldson referred to him as an eccentric relative, and the two endlessly sniped at each other, a procession of verbal darts, like a marriage that had lasted too long.

During one game the year before, Bluto had sat in the front row, and at one quiet moment during a foul shot, yelled out at Donaldson, "Way to go, Turk. No points. No rebounds."

We all had our own shelf in the kitchen. Purvis had boxes of rice. Donaldson's was empty. As was mine. Bluto's was stocked with enough provisions to survive a nuclear attack.

He loved to come out into the living room with a tray full of cold cuts and a large kitchen knife. He would put a piece of meat at the end of the knife, then make languorous faces as he slowly ate the meat off the knife, as if this was the most sensual and satisfying experience of his life. By now, Donaldson would be almost salivating, inevitably would make a grab for one of the cold cuts, a move that found Bluto with the knife quickly up to Donaldson's throat.

"Keep your hands off my stuff," he warned, "or I'll slit your throat. I'll slice you like a bluefish."

Most of the time we thought he was kidding, of course; some nights we weren't too sure.

Our ritual was almost always the same. We would watch the *Tonight Show,* then a late TV movie, then drive down the hill into downtown Providence to one of the two lunch carts that were open all night across from the old gray City Hall that squatted at the front of Kennedy Plaza. Then it was over to the train station to play "the genius game," trivia questions that Bluto and Donaldson would haggle over, before getting back to the apartment about three and sleeping until the late morning.

One winter night, in the middle of downtown at three in the morning, Donaldson wasn't wearing a coat.

"Where's your coat?" Bluto asked.

"Only wimps like you need a coat," Donaldson said.

"Fuck you, you ugly Turk," Bluto countered.

They continued to banter, another skirmish in their constant sparring, until Donaldson claimed he could run back to the apartment in only his underwear, forget the cold. Bluto bet him he couldn't, and off Donaldson went, running through the night. He ran up College Hill as we followed him in Bluto's pale blue Volvo, then through streets as quiet as the inside of a tomb. At the top of our street Donaldson took off his underwear and sprinted nude down the middle of the street, his arms thrown over his head in triumph, as though he were winning the Boston Marathon.

It seemed a fitting symbol for the way we lived. The country was going through cataclysmic shocks that would change it forever; we were acting like fifteen-year-olds at summer camp.

Basketball was the only thing that gave our lives some organization. Every afternoon there was practice, the promise of another season. It gave the day a sense of purpose. We were seniors now, Donaldson, Landau, Sigur, myself, the last four remaining from that freshman class in the fall of 1964. This was going to be the year that redeemed us as a team, the one that lived up to the collective promise we had shown as freshmen.

Or so we liked to think.

6

I had no idea what lay beyond basketball on that February night on the bus back from Princeton in the winter of 1968. It had been my identity for too long, had defined me in so many ways.

A couple of weeks earlier, on a similar bus trip to upstate New York to play Cornell, I had stumbled across a *Sports Illustrated* article by Jack Kerouac, the chronicler of the Beat Generation whose *On the Road* would soon be rediscovered and treated like a long-lost artifact. I knew virtually nothing about Kerouac at the time, knew nothing about the Beat Movement other than that they supposedly wore black all the time and looked a lot like the greasers and "mondoes" who used to hang out in front of Rod's Grille in Warren back in high school. That and the Maynard G. Krebs character on the old Dobie Gillis television show who used to say "man" a lot and act weird.

The article was excerpted from Kerouac's *Vanity of Du-louz*, and was about the short time Kerouac had spent as a football player at Columbia in the late forties. Seems he'd been a high-school football star in Lowell, Massachusetts, a bleak old mill town north of Boston, promising enough to be recruited by Columbia and sent to a year of prep school at Horace Mann in New York City. The gist of the article was how disillusioned Kerouac had been at Columbia, had come to realize that all the Ivy League really was was "an excuse to get football players for nothing."

Outside of the obvious similarities in our experiences, I was struck by how Kerouac had asked himself many of the same questions I was starting to ask that night on the bus coming back on the bus from Princeton when I first began to question the one-dimensional way I had grown up, to question the all-encompassing power of sports. What had this all been for? Was there a future without basketball?

Questions I had no answers for.

The season ended about a month later. Ironically, I began playing better after that night on the bus, the best basketball of my career. By this point I had such confidence in my shooting ability that I thought I was never going to miss. The only problem was getting the shots off. Hounded by the other team's best defensive guard, players invariably more athletic than I was, I often resorted to twisting, fall-away jumpers just to get shots off. I averaged over twenty points a game in those last weeks of my career, once making the weekly All-East team. But it was never enough, not really. We were still a mediocre team, nothing more, still a team going nowhere, lodged in the Ivy League's second division.

The league was simply too tough for us. Princeton, even with Bradley gone three years now, was still one of the top teams in the country, complete with two players who would later play in the NBA, Ed Hummer and Geoff Petrie. Columbia had Jim McMillian, who later played for years in the NBA, and a seven-foot center in Dave Newmark. Columbia also had beat a Louisville team that featured Wes Unseld and Butch Beard to win the Holiday Festival in Madison Square Garden. Cornell had beaten Kentucky in Lexington the year before, with a great player named Gregory Morris, a quick black kid whose athleticism reemphasized our own limitations.

"I can't even dribble on the same court as him," Donaldson muttered, after one horrible road trip to Cornell and Columbia, back-to-back disasters. "I traveled a hundred miles to score four points."

All year we had confronted the overpowering awareness that we were not as good as we wanted to be, both individually and collectively. It was not an easy acknowledgment. We all had put so much time into it, so much of our identity. I had been on a team since I was in the seventh grade. Being a player was all I knew, the way I measured my life, the way I perceived both the world and my place in it.

We had begun the season with the dreams all teams have, each year a clean slate upon which to write a new script. Now we limped to the finish like some old horse yearning for the barn, worn down, playing out the string, waiting for the end.

Ever since that night at Princeton when Geoff Petrie had tooled me, letting me see firsthand my athletic mortality, I had come to resent basketball. Not the game itself, but the entire jock culture that surrounded it. The simplistic slogans that hung on the locker-room walls. The traditional way sports defined masculinity. The one-dimensional nature of sports.

The obsession with winning. I resented the fact that I had been naive enough to swallow all of it, to believe that if you wanted something badly enough, lusted after it long enough, it would happen, the message I had grown up hearing from a succession of coaches. I had believed in that most American of beliefs, that all dreams come true if you only work hard enough.

That one game had punctured that myth as dramatically as a knife punctures a childhood balloon. Reality in the guise of a jump shot in your face.

Most of all, I resented all the time spent, the steep price of obsession. What could my life have been if I had never played? How different would it be?

The last game was against Providence College in their Alumni Hall, the citadel of dreams for a Rhode Island kid, the one place I always had wanted to play in. It had been the place where we had played the state tournament my junior year in high school, back when we upset LaSalle and carried Cronin off the court, the biggest win we ever had. Now it was six years later, and everything was so different.

I sat by myself in the locker room before the game, thinking of all the locker rooms I had sat in, trying to remember them. I knew it would be the last game I would ever play in, and I wanted to remember everything about it, the anxiety in my stomach, the sweat rolling down my arms, the dryness in my throat, the feeling that I was about to do something so very important. In some perverse sense, I had come to love these sensations, like old friends who always showed up. I wanted to freeze-frame everything, sensing that it would be important later. I knew that I would never be a pro, never play again in a real game, never again sit in a locker room with my stomach in knots. All the years and all the practice; all the

wishing and hoping and yearning that had started out in the
driveway so many years before; all the bus rides and sprained
ankles—all of it, had brought me to this place. This locker
room. This game.

The end of the trail.

Like virtually all the games I played in I remember almost
none of the details, as though the actual games took place in
some other consciousness, some other realm. We got beat, a
game that never was really close, and I didn't play particularly
well. All athletes dream of ending their career being carried off
the court on the shoulders of their teammates, the big cine-
matic moment. Being carried off, cutting down the net, the
hero's farewell, just like that prep-school year at Worcester
Academy had ended. But it hadn't been that way in high
school, and didn't end that way now. There was no Hollywood ending. Just the buzzer going off.

Yet afterward in the locker room I felt none of the usual
postgame malaise after a loss. None of the self-examination,
the questioning, the sense of failure. Instead, there was a sense
of relief, as though some lead weight had been lifted.

The spring of 1968.

A high-school friend already had been killed in Vietnam, his
body sent home in a casket wrapped in the American flag.
The weekly peace vigils on the campus green grew larger and
larger. The war, the draft, and the uncertainty of the future
seemed to inevitably to creep into every conversation. Donaldson talked of maybe going to Canada to escape the draft;
he was morally opposed to fighting in Vietnam. Bluto still
talked of wanting to "go kill gooks," had spent much of the
year walking by the peace vigils on the college green, ranting

about the "peace creeps" and "flits," looking for any opportunity to punch one of them out.

I felt lost in the middle somewhere. My student deferment was going to end in June, regardless of the fact that I wasn't going to graduate, would still be two courses short. I already had been to a pre-induction physical, the first step in being drafted.

One day I went to an old brick armory in Pawtucket, the old mill city that adjoined Providence to the north. There was a National Guard unit there with a basketball team. The word was they were looking for players, even if it was virtually impossible to get into the National Guard then, so coveted were the spots. The sergeant was stocky, balding, dressed in fatigues. He sat behind a gray desk in a small room with recruiting pictures on the walls.

"You're the guy from Brown, right?" he said, looking me over. "The shooter."

He talked about how the unit already had some good players, naming some familiar names from my high-school days. Then he pulled out several papers stapled together, all with names in small print on them. It was the waiting list, the one that determined who got to sit out the war at home going to drills and playing soldier once a month, and who was undoubtedly going to get drafted.

"I don't know," I said, pointing to the list. "I'm getting out of school in June."

"Don't worry," he said. "I'm putting you third."

Two weeks later I was in.

Basketball had helped me again. Even if I had come to resent it.

Not that I had any clue about what I wanted to do with my life.

So many of the guys I knew at Brown were either going off to graduate school or going to some inner city to teach; both were ways to escape the draft. To many of them, law school or business school was one more stop on the way station to the seductive promise of an Ivy League education, the last part of the plan that already had been in place when they entered college. To me, the future was still as blurry and unfocused as it always had been, save for my father's vision that once you graduate from college you go off and get some good job in corporate America.

Just what was that good job?

Who knew.

The only thing I knew was what I didn't want to do. That had been reinforced one sunny spring afternoon during an interview at a Providence insurance company, when I had found myself sitting in front of a varnished desk in a blue blazer and gray slacks, looking like some backup singer for Pat Boone. It all seemed like an alien world: the men in their dark business suits; the secretaries in their stockings and heels; the man behind the desk who gave me one of those handshakes that could bring a wrestler to his knees.

"So why do you think you might want to sell insurance?" he said in a voice so smooth it sounded silky.

I don't, I wanted to say. *I would rather do anything but sell insurance.*

I felt like I had that day at Exeter when I had been asked what "periodicals" were.

Instead, I mumbled some banalities about wanting a career where I could work with people, hollow words from some script someone must have given me. I didn't want to sell insurance. Didn't want to sell anything. What I wanted to do was go off somewhere and have all the experiences I felt basketball had prevented. Like David Janssen in *The Fugitive*, the ultimate loner who always was on the move from the law, all the while looking for the one-armed man who had killed his wife. Or Ben Gazzara in *Run for Your Life*, who, while dying of a terminal disease, kept going to exotic places where sultry women always were falling for him, attracted to his sense of mystery, his remoteness, the fact he was different.

These were my cultural role models. Right there with Steve McQueen and Paul Newman and all the other existential heroes I instinctively related to. They always played loners, men just passing through, piling up experiences like points in a basketball game, points to be tabulated later. Men who seemed to exist on the outside of the system, living by some personal code. Like Donaldson who said he wanted to go to New York and live with a hooker. He was going to teach in a Brooklyn ghetto. No selling insurance. No corporate America for him.

Or for me, either.

So I went back to Barrington for the summer, waiting to go away for basic training, a six-month stint in the regular army before coming back to Rhode Island to attend monthly National Guard drills. Only this time it was different. No daily shooting on the court across the street from the high school. No summer league. No pickup games. No thinking about next season. No basketball at all. I saw all that as belonging to the past, something to be stored away in some childhood footlocker, right there with my scrapbooks.

Sarles got married that summer, to a girl he had met while he was at Amherst. Raffa and I went to the wedding. It was held in a Boston suburb on a warm summer morning. There were only a handful of people there from Barrington, and already there was the very clear sense that Jay's life was moving in a different direction. Then again, we always had known it would.

Pat Monti got married that summer, to a girl he'd gone out with all through high school, a former cheerleader. Raffa was planning to get married in December, to the younger sister of a girl we knew in high school. Dinah was working in Germany. My mother was planning to sell the house, move to Cape Cod to work for her brother-in-law. Everything was changing, the past crumbling, like a foundation no longer capable of supporting the structure above it.

I started to read. First it was *On the Road,* then all of Kerouac I could find: *The Dharma Bums, Desolation Angels, Big Sur.* I began to identify with the Beats, their antimaterialism, their rejection of corporate America and the mindless conformity they supposedly saw all around them. Instead, I dreamed of taking off, of seeing other places, like George Maharis and Martin Milner used to do in the old television show *Route 66.*

"Come on," I said to Raffa. "Let's drive across the country. One last fling before you get married."

"Yeah," he said. "We'll drive all night and sleep on the beach all day."

"There are no beaches in Iowa," I said.

"Then why go?" he said.

Raffa was ever the pragmatist.

His wife-to-be didn't want him to leave. She wanted him to start acting like an adult, not go off cross-country with me, as if we were still in high school driving around town talking about the upcoming season. He had a job lined up at a small private school in Barrington for kids with social problems. He wanted to coach, had always wanted to coach.

I wanted to take off to the sky.

My girlfriend thought I was getting weird. Her name was

Sue, she had honey-colored hair, and she was the first girl since Dinah I was serious about. We had been going out for over a year and there were times I wanted to marry her, for it still seemed as if that's what you did when you got out of college. I could close my eyes and see us living together, building a life, coming home from some job every day to have her meet me by the door, dinner simmering on the stove, like a scene from *Leave It to Beaver*. Just what I was supposed to be doing during the day was a little unclear. Sue was younger than me, though, still had three years of college left, and her parents viewed me as too old. Little did they know.

Still, our worlds were growing farther apart. Her aspirations were rooted in her reality. She wanted to finish school, get married, live the kind of suburban, monied life she'd been raised to live, the replication of her childhood. I was the one with the unfocused dreams, the adolescent longings, the yearning for a world I knew nothing about. The one who wasn't sure if there was a life beyond basketball.

It was a yearning that took me through basic training at Fort Gordon, Georgia, the following fall, where for the first time it didn't matter that I had a jump shot. Didn't matter who I knew, or what I did, or where I had gone to college, or who I was. None of it mattered. I was just another recruit with a shaved head and dressed in green fatigues, no different than all the others. We lived in a barracks, complete with inspections and fire watches and punishment for everything from a sloppily made bed to poorly shined shoes. We got up every morning at four-thirty, aided by a drill sergeant who burst through the door wearing fatigues and a brown wide-brimmed Smokey the Bear hat, shouting for us to get our sorry, tired asses out

of bed. Then it was outside the barracks for the first formation of the day, followed by calisthenics in the red dust. To get
inside the cafeteria you had to go through the monkey bars
first.

It soon took on its own reality, a tiny insular world of
marching and training, far removed from anything that was
taking place outside the gates of Fort Gordon. We were exempt
from everything, purposely so. No newspapers. No television.
No radio. Nothing except the daily attempt to transform us
into soldiers, many of whom would eventually be headed for
Vietnam. It was a long way from all those peace vigils on the
Brown campus the year before.

We learned how to fight with bayonets. We learned how to
fight hand-to-hand. We learned how to shoot M-16 weapons.
We learned how to stand in formation. Most of all, we learned
how to march. From the parade grounds at the end of the
street, to the rifle ranges on the periphery of the base, we always were marching somewhere. Often, we would march for
what seemed like hours, past the white barracks and the
parched fields and the banks of red clay, would march to the
middle of nowhere, only to stop. Stop and sit there doing
nothing to the point that eventually it became obvious that no
one knew where we were, or what we were supposed to be
doing.

"No wonder the Viet Cong is winning," a kid yelled from
the back.

Or else we would have to lie on the ground with both our
feet and legs in the air. The "dying cockroach" position.

"That's what you pukes are," the drill sergeant said, the
words all but snapping through his teeth. "As worthless as
dying cockroaches."

He had a toothpick in the side of his mouth, a perpetual

sneer on his face. He looked at us through eyes that had squinted across innumerable parched parade fields, didn't like what he saw.

"Are you tough, boy?" he yelled, his face an inch a way from some recruit. "Are you tough, boy?"

"Yes, Drill Sergeant," the kid said, his voice almost quavering. The kid was about eighteen, right out of some backwoods high school, in way over his head.

"Tough enough to jump into Vietnam?" the drill sergeant barked. "Tough enough to be an Army Ranger?"

"Yes, Drill Sergeant."

"We'll see, now won't we, boy," the drill sergeant said, spitting on the ground for emphasis.

It was all intimidation, and it worked. Most of the guys in the barracks were eighteen, uneducated, already on the assembly line that invariably would take them to Vietnam. But there were a half dozen of us, out of college, all going home when our six-month active-duty stint was over. The drill sergeants had little power over us, other than their ability to make each day miserable.

"Are you tough, boy?" the drill sergeant asked me one morning.

"No, Drill Sergeant."

He was visibly taken aback.

"What do you mean you're not tough?" he said, putting his face right into mine.

"I'm not particularly tough," I said.

He stared at me, shook his head in obvious disgust, and walked away. Then he turned around and came back to my face, again staring.

"You just don't give a shit, do you?" he finally said.

The next stop was Fort Rucker, Alabama, for on-the-job

training as a military policeman. I spent the days cruising through the scrub pine of the base in a dark green police sedan, .45-caliber weapon at my right side, past places called Tank Hill and Copter Corner. The bullets always were in my left pocket, for fear I'd shoot myself in the foot by mistake.

On Sunday mornings we took the prisoners to church, sat in the pews while they were handcuffed to us. They were mostly kids, younger than I was, their crimes usually nothing more than going AWOL, absent without leave. I felt sorry for them. They seemed so lost, scared kids away from home, dragged into a war they neither wanted nor understood.

The war was always a presence. In basic training there had been constant reminders. Everything was geared to move people through basic training quickly, the first step on the treadmill to Southeast Asia. Yet there also were hints of how barbaric the war there actually was, whether it was a sergeant who bragged of pushing Viet Cong out of helicopters if they didn't talk, or others who had been there letting us know that what was going on was too grisly to even talk about.

One night shortly before Christmas a sergeant came into the barracks, drunk and raging. He was one of those lifers, career soldiers with skin haircuts, the ones who always were calling us pussies and queers and pukes. The ones who gave off the impression that there was nothing more noble in the entire world than to jump out of a plane into Vietnam. The kind of soldier who seemed to have stepped out of the pages of a comic book. Now, though, he was all too human, and not caring who knew it.

"I don't want to go back," he said, punching the wall. "They can't make me go back."

After that night I didn't need some antiwar protester to tell me how bad the war was.

But if active duty was mindless, something to be endured, not understood, it changed me.

For the first time in my life I felt what it meant to be truly powerless, to be the victim of your own status, without any hope or chance that the situation could be rectified. For the first time I was faceless, part of the *lumpenprole* of recruits, as indistinguishable as sheep. I have never looked at power the same way since.

*So when I began teaching at Barrington High School the fol-*lowing fall I was as different as the school. No longer were athletes the undisputed kings, no longer did they roam the halls like young princes inside some walled city, as we had done only six years earlier. Now they competed with the counterculture kids, the so-called freaks, with their long hair and their bell-bottoms and their open disdain for everything that was traditional. The school had become a microcosm of society: two disparate groups staring at each other from a distance. I was hired to be an English teacher and assistant basketball coach. The people who hired me thought I wanted to be the basketball coach. They were wrong. I wanted to be the teacher, even though I never had taken any education classes, or student-taught, or done anything but substitute.

And I figured I only had one message to teach the kids who sat there in front of me: Don't do what I have done. Don't grow up one-dimensional. Don't grow up thinking the world ends at the East Providence line. Explore things. Be open to the possibilities.

They, of course, didn't want to hear it. Most of them, anyway. Bored by a curriculum that hadn't changed in decades, chafing under rules that treated them as if they were ten years old, many of them were as lost as I had been at their age.

"Can I go to the lav?" one kid asked.

"Do what you want to do," I said quickly. "I get paid either way."

I had little use for the endless permission slips and corridor passes. Or for the curriculum that was as heavy and dusty as an old attic. The kids had old textbooks. The first story in one of them was *Beowulf,* the tale that had bludgeoned generations of high-school students. We started reading it and you could see the eyes start to glaze over, mine included. I was supposed to teach this? That night I went to a bookstore and bought twenty-five copies of *The Catcher in the Rye,* sensing that if they didn't like the story of an alienated adolescent who thought all adults were phonies, we might as well close the school and turn it into a warehouse.

"All right, let's be honest, who likes *Beowulf?*" I asked.

No one raised his hand.

"Okay, pass them up."

So began my career as a teacher. I quickly learned that it was all about the cult of personality, the ability to get kids to listen, to keep them interested. Without that, everything else was irrelevant. That, and making them think you were crazier than they were.

"What's your problem, Victor?" I asked a slight kid with long hair that often fell across his face. He had been an irritant for a couple of weeks, one of those kids who sat in the back, slouched in his seat, his face locked in a perpetual sneer, making comments under his breath at every opportunity. Now we were outside in the corridor, and he was up against the locker, with my hand against his chest. I hadn't heard of the ACLU back then.

"I don't like school," he said.

"You don't have to like school," I said. "But we're going to get something resolved right here. Me and you. You get it? Because you're not going to bust my balls anymore. And if you do, then I'm going to bust yours, and I promise you're not going to like that. You get what I'm saying to you?"

I knew Victor was afraid of me, something I was not averse to using to my advantage. I also knew he was surprised by my language. Advantage number two.

"You like cars, right?"

He nodded.

"Do you know how to fix them?"

He nodded again.

"Okay, here's the deal," I said. "You don't bust my balls and I won't bust yours. You fix my car if it breaks down, and I pass you. Think it over."

Victor didn't think long.

"That's cool," he said.

I already had learned that reaching kids is all about improvising. Save the pedagogy for the education classes.

Henry taught social studies. He, too, was in his first year. He, too, had been a high-school basketball player, a couple of years ahead of me, had played on a Providence high-school team that won a state championship. He, too, had put the game behind him.

He lived with his wife in a small house he rented in Barrington across the street from the old Little League field. On the living room wall was a huge poster of Che Guevara. His German shepherd also was named Che. Henry wore wire-rim ⟩ glasses and had black hair that fell over his collar in the back, hair that framed a thin intense face. He spoke rapidly, his arms serving as punctuation marks, his words all but tumbling over themselves trying to get out of his mouth. He didn't so much talk to people as verbally attack them. He reminded me of how Kerouac had described Dean Moriarty in *On the Road*, someone who never yawned or said a commonplace thing, but "burned burned burned like some fabulous Roman candle."

Shortly after we met we went out one night, along with Henry's wife and another teacher. We had been to a raucous party in Providence, full of too many drinks and too much marijuana, and by the end of the evening Henry was very drunk. On the way home, at a traffic light on Providence's East Side, only a few blocks from Brown, Henry inexplicably jumped out of the car and started running down a side street.

"What's he doing?" his wife wailed, near hysteria.

I had no idea and took off after him.

Henry was around the corner, standing in an alley.

"I'm not going to die in Providence, Rhode Island," he said, as I approached him. "I'm going to die in the sands of San Francisco."

Oh.

Henry had grown up in the Smith Hill section of Providence, a working-class neighborhood of wooden three-decker tenements where even the dogs wore the look of poverty. He had used basketball to escape and go to college. But he had never forgotten his roots and the too-many dreams he had seen die in the deadening jobs and the neighborhood bars. Now he carried a class-consciousness around with him like a weapon. To him, life was a morality play, a struggle between capitalism and the proletariat, simply an outgrowth of his Smith Hill youth when he and his friends used to go to the parties of their more affluent high-school classmates and steal pocketbooks. The only difference was, now he had the theoretical ammunition to back up his instincts.

He talked endlessly of social justice, of the growing Movement that was going to end the war and transform America into a worker's paradise. He subscribed to innumerable leftist periodicals like *Ramparts* and *Evergreen Review.* Henry didn't just read Marx. He had note cards on him. He read many of the Eastern European Marxists, kept the notes in notebooks he stored in file cabinets, file cabinets he treated as if they contained the secrets of the universe. He read Marcuse. He read C. Wright Mills. He read Emma Goldman. He pored over his periodicals, studied them, devoured them, made them articles of his faith.

He never talked about his basketball, as if he had moved so far beyond it that it had happened to someone else. His politics had replaced his basketball, had become a new competitive arena.

On the day he was going to first meet his future father-in-law, a professor at a local college, he studied all afternoon.

"I'm going to be ready," he said.

"For what?" I asked.

"For anything," he said. "I'm not going in there unprepared."

But he was full of contradictions, too, wonderful contradictions. For all his political sensitivity, he loved possessions, especially elaborate sound systems for his music.

"Nothing too good for the working class," he said to any criticism of his outward displays of materialism.

He sat in the teachers' room that first fall, as the leaves began to change out past the football field, and threw verbal footballs at the other teachers. In his view, life was a battle, every conversation a skirmish. An ongoing skirmish, like some game that never ended.

One summer he stayed in his house and studied all day. His wife wanted to go to the beach, do normal things. Henry studied. All day. Every day. Studied and took notes. He poured all of his energy into mastering this new material. The marriage became strained. Henry said it was because his wife didn't read enough. So he gave her a reading list, made her promise to read for at least an hour every night, heavy political tomes. Still, Henry burned like some Roman candle.

But it wasn't just Henry.

Abe was in his forties, a large, rugged man who looked like the actor Hugh O'Brien. He had been teaching for nearly twenty years. Once he had taught me in junior high, had even been my junior-high football coach, on a team that failed to win a game and ended any thought of me being a high-school quarterback. He'd been the assistant football coach at Barrington High School for years, but when the head coach had retired, Abe had been passed over for the top job, a slight that seemed to change his life. He had been the loyal soldier, believing in the system. He had grown up poor and fatherless, had worked hard his entire life, believing that hard work ultimately would be rewarded. Salt of the earth, Henry called him, the kind of guy who would give you the shirt off his back. Now Abe felt betrayed, and it made him challenge everything. The school system. The town. The country. His life.

Henry quickly became his mentor. Henry's political philosophy was a theoretical foundation for Abe's malaise. Soon Abe began wearing blue workshirts to school, saying he was a "worker" and he was only wearing something appropriate, a fashion statement considered heresy within the school. Male teachers were still expected to wear jackets and ties. Even the occasional turtleneck was seen as some form of countercultural statement. Abe took it to another dimension. Most of his colleagues looked at him as though he'd had a breakdown.

By this time he was living in one room in his basement. It was spartan, only a small cot, a reading lamp, an endless supply of books. His wife and children lived upstairs, living symbols of the life he was quickly outgrowing, like old clothes from some other era.

"I'm on a journey," he said. "I just don't know where it's going to lead."

None of us did.

There was a woman teacher who came to school stoned every morning, moved through the day in a personal trance. One Monday morning, after hearing me complain I was tired from the weekend, she gave me a tiny pill.

"This will perk you up," she said.

I didn't sleep for two days, hated the sensation of my body tuned to a different speed.

There was Stan, who one night discovered his wife was having an affair and went to the man's apartment with a gun, planning to kill both of them, then himself. But he fell asleep in the car.

"To this day I don't know whether I should be grateful I fell asleep or not," he said. Periodically, he would drop to the floor of his classroom and do push-ups. If a female student asked him how he was doing, he would pretend to cough and say, "Horny."

There was Aaron who had gone to Brown a couple of years behind me. He was tall and lanky, with bushy hair and wire-rim glasses. When he laughed his entire body convulsed. He laughed often. To him, standing in front of a classful of suburban faces was his idea of a cosmic joke. He often came into class, took off his sports jacket, and threw it on the floor in a symbol of bourgeois defiance. One night early in his teaching career Aaron showed up at a party Henry was having for the people in his department. The only problem was Aaron showed up with war paint all over his face.

"What are you, crazy?" Henry said to him. "These are the straightest people on the planet in here."

"Sorry," Aaron said. "I forgot the stuff was still on my face. I just came from an acid party at Brown."

I liked them all for many reasons, not least that they had nothing to do with basketball. They did not know me as a basketball player, nor did they care that I once had played. With them, I had a clean page upon which to write a new story.

It was all one big freak show. We were intoxicated by ideas, by new books, by the sense that everything was in flux, changing into who-knew-what. Something dramatic was happening and we all had a chance to be a part of it. I woke up in the morning excited about going off to teach, excited about this new part of my life that seemed to offer so many possibilities.

We were young and always would be. And the very worst thing was growing old—old being synomous with corruption, people who had bought into the materialism of a country that had lost its soul. Or so the party line went.

"Old man, take a look at my life," Neil Young sang. *"Twenty-four and there's so much more."*

I was twenty-four too. With the same attitude.

It's easy to misinterpret the sixties now, to cloak them in romanticism, see them in simplistic terms, as an ongoing countercultural party with its pronouncements of peace and love and the dawning of the Age of Aquarius. It was more complicated than that, and came with a hard edge. It was too much change too soon, the fallout of which irreparably changed the country. It wasn't just the drugs, though that was a large part of it. It was the sense that everything became polarized, political correctness before anyone knew what the term meant. Everything was black or white. You were either for the war or against it. You were either for the legalization of marijuana, or you weren't. You were either for the counterculture and all the baggage that went with it, or you weren't. You were either young or old, on this side or that side. There was no in-between, no shades of gray. The battle lines were drawn in the sand and fiercely defended, and by the early seventies it had all turned ugly.

"Where have all the flowers gone?"

No one seemed to know anymore.

I saw it with the kids I taught. They fell into three groups: the "freaks" with their counterculture accoutrements; the "socially aware" kids who were trying to make some sense of a world that seemed to be coming apart at the seams; the jocks and cheerleaders with their traditional values, as if they had gone to high school with me six years ago.

No matter that most of them had grown up with each other, come of age together. There was little room for compromise, no sense that things might be more complicated than they appeared on the surface. You were either with us, or you weren't. It was easy then to look at a classroom of kids and, with too few exceptions, know what they felt about everything simply by what clothes they wore and how long their hair was. It was not the easiest time to come of age.

I also saw it with the kids I coached.

Basketball, like the other sports, no longer was an end in itself, as it once had been. It, too, was now politicized. To play sports was to make a statement, the inference being that you supported the war, believed in traditional values. Basketball at Barrington High School had changed dramatically during the seven years since I had played; the teams no longer were as good, the crowds had shrunk, there wasn't the sense that the entire school was behind us. In many ways basketball had become just another activity.

Not that I was a particularly good coach. It was the wrong time in my life. My heart wasn't in it. I didn't want to be in the gym where the banners from the past hung on the walls, the same gym where so many of my best memories were; it was like sitting in your childhood home that's now lived in by some other family. It also was a bizarre time to be a coach. Sports were under such attack. Things that once had been taken for granted, things like discipline and selflessness, were now seen as belonging to some prehistoric age.

In the middle of a game a girl crawled in front of me, squeezed between the bench and the court.

"What do you think you're doing?" I asked.

"I'm going to see Kevin," she said.

Oh.

One night, on a bus ride to some high school in the northern part of the state, we got lost on narrow, tenement-lined streets. It was snowing outside, the bus full of teenage chatter. I felt as if I was drowning. This is what I was trying to get away from.

I often talked to my friends of how destructive competition was, how it was merely one more negative example of a capitalist society that pitted people against each other, and how everything would be better if people could learn to cooperate with each other instead of compete. I even believed it. Yet I didn't want to have a kid beat me in a shooting game after practice. I often talked about how sports placed too much emphasis on winning. Yet when the games started, I wanted to win as a coach, just as I always had wanted to win as a player.

"See that coach over there?" I said minutes before a game, pointing to the opposing coach, as the jayvee team gathered around me. Once, the other coach had been a high-school rival. Now he looked like he'd grown up on Carnaby Street: Beatle boots, granny glasses, bell-bottoms. "See that guy? He looks like Bozo the Clown and I don't want to lose to him, okay?"

It wasn't exactly *"Win one for the Gipper,"* but my team loved it. They broke from the huddle with a surge of energy. Win one for the coach who doesn't want to lose to Bozo the Clown.

They went out and lost anyway.

I quit coaching after the second year, went back to my self-imposed exile from the game. I saw it as one more example of my evolution, the game receding farther and farther back into the distance. I also saw it as liberating. There would be no thought of me being the next Barrington coach, no more pretense. *The game has nothing to do with me anymore,* I told myself.

Henry and I went to Europe that summer. I saw it as one more conscious effort to distance myself from the game. Henry was separated from his wife, and his fantasy was to stay in Europe, eventually going to some socialist country, so he had all his personal papers with him. First we had to take a bus to New York, from where the flight to London would leave.

"Let's walk through Times Square," he said, as we arrived at the Port Authority bus station. "I want to walk through the belly of the beast one more time. To say good-bye to the soul of capitalism."

It was a scorching July afternoon. We walked down 42nd Street with packs on our backs, past the peep shows and the hustlers and the rows of movie marquees, the Great White Way in all its seedy tarnish.

"I can't live here anymore," Henry said, almost to himself.

We landed in London the next morning, began a three-week odyssey through Europe. To Pamplona to run with the bulls. To the French Riviera, where the beach was dirty, the women were topless, and decadence hung in the air like coastal fog. To Geneva and Munich. We traveled by train, slept in crummy places, even outside in a public park in Munich. It was a summer of a profusion of American youth traveling through Europe, all with packs on their backs, a whole generation of Dharma Bums, all in search of something that supposedly had been lost in America. They were everywhere, in every train station, every tourist attraction, as if London were just New York with double-decker buses. Henry had a visceral hatred of them. To him, they were a part of America he was trying to escape from. He viewed them as trendy, cultural instead of political.

"Suburban revolutionaries," he snorted. "Che Guevara goes to the mall."

We went from country to country, from city to city, looking for who-knows-what. Some romanticized vision of Europe? Someplace that wasn't America? All of the above? In a sense we were both running, Henry toward some worker's paradise, me away from a past I didn't understand.

Eventually, we got to Heidelberg where Dinah was living, teaching at the large American army base on the outskirts of town. I hadn't seen her in a couple of years, but we still had so many unresolved questions between us. I was excited about seeing her, but anxious too.

We went to her apartment. Her German boyfriend was there, along with several others. His name was Wolfgang. He was blond and burly with a haughty manner. Dinah told me he didn't like most Americans. She seemed happy to see me, but it was awkward too. We were so far away from those nights in high school. It was late at night. We sat in her bedroom and talked, as I tried to impress upon her that I no longer was the one-dimensional basketball player she had once known, but some sort of politically aware, quasi-Bohemian, *blah, blah, blah*. It was all bittersweet. We were linked together, yet such a product of a different time, a certain innocence that was as over as poodle skirts and penny loafers. Perhaps Dinah always had known this, ever since she first went away to college and sensed that we were finished, forever locked in a certain time and place, Barrington in the early 1960s, a time that couldn't sustain itself.

I suppose I wanted some sort of validation, some sign from her that she had made a big mistake by dumping me and had come to regret it. Not that I would have known what to do with that sort of declaration, but I wanted it nonetheless. Instead, she talked about Europe, how liberating it was, how free she felt to be so far away from home, family, and a country she felt she'd outgrown. The more she talked the more I realized that with Dinah I was still playing catch-up, and always would be.

In the next room we could hear loud voices arguing.

There in the middle of the living room Henry and Wolfgang were rolling on the floor, shouting heated words and pushing each other, an argument gone too far.

"All Germans are closet fascists," Henry said minutes later.

Dinah walked us to the door. She was upset. Wolfgang was still hollering in the next room about how all Americans were assholes. Henry wanted to go back and sucker-punch him. I felt I never would see Dinah again, that we had too much tortured history between us, that every time we met we only pulled farther apart.

Within a year she would be back in Barrington recovering from a serious brain operation, for an aneuryism that burst in her head when she climbed out of a swimming pool. But back then I touched her lightly on the cheek and walked away, trying to be studly, as in some scene from *The Fugitive*. I didn't look back and she didn't say a word.

The next morning Henry and I were on another train, heading off to some other supposed adventure. This time it was Amsterdam, the hippie paradise, where we would smoke dope in Dam Square among a microcosm of the world's counterculture littering the streets and canals of a beautiful city that believed so fervently in personal freedom and now was seeing the price tag for that belief. We arrived there at midnight in a drizzle. Down the street from the train station was an Orange Julius stand. A Neil Diamond song was on the radio, all about how *"I am lost and I don't even know why."*

This was Europe?

We got a room in a run-down pension. The next morning we went outside and discovered we were in the middle of the "red light" district, almost-naked women sitting in windows, a horde of tourists in the street. A socialist paradise? It all seemed like Times Square.

That night we went to a club. Across the street there were several guys openly selling marijuana and hash. The room was incredibly loud, too crowded, the music whipping everyone into a frenzy. One of the band members was holding up a skull. The lead singer was a small woman with dark hair. Henry said she reminded him of his ex-wife. Eventually he freaked out and we ended up outside.

We sat on a bench across the street, feeling far from home.

Henry had believed so much in the Movement, the potential for the counterculture to change society. It was a concept that had started with promise, born in the civil-rights movement, later coalescing into the antiwar movement. The music, the clothes, the sexual freedom, the drugs—they all had been a part of it, but, in Henry's view, never the most important part. To him, the soul of the Movement was its political base, the belief that the social system had to fundamentally change. That had been the article of his faith, and now he saw it all being co-opted, rock music being used to sell products, the political core becoming rotten from too many drugs and too much hedonism, the promise already sullied.

Tonight had merely been the exclamation point, as though he had seen the future and it wasn't going to be good.

"Let's go home," he said sadly.

To another year.

Another year without the game that once had defined me.

Every once in a while I would get a clue that something was missing, something deep and important, but I didn't know what it was. I came to view these moments as little more than remnants of nostalgia, like driving by Dinah's house, or the house on the corner of Bluff Road and Governor Bradford Drive I had grown up in, memories of a childhood that was gone forever.

The last thing I wanted to be was some ex-jock who sat

around talking about the big game, as though life had stopped in high school, like Rabbit Angstrom in John Updike's *Rabbit Run*. Reading that book was like running into a blind pick: the small town with its built-in provincialism, the high-school scoring star and the feeling that nothing could ever match that buzz, a life that had unraveled, split like some old basketball.

"American lives don't have any second acts," Fitzgerald wrote.

I was going to be different, I told myself. I just wasn't sure what that second act would be.

So everything became geared to having experiences, as if life was one giant hole that you could never fill up. It was my way of rationalizing, the simplistic thinking that no experience was a bad one as long as you learned something from it, as long as it took you somewhere. In a sense an entire generation was starting to do that, symbolically trying on new clothes. New fashions, new ideas. New everything.

There was a girl who drove from Providence to the West Coast with her cat because she wanted to see the Pacific Ocean. She drove three thousand miles across the country, went to Venice Beach, walked into the water to her knees, then got back into the car and began driving back. There were guys I had known all my life who suddenly looked like the Beatles on *Sergeant Pepper*, complete with long hair and handlebar mustaches.

"There's something happening here. What it is ain't exactly clear."

Now I know that many of the things I did then stemmed from some unconscious desire to fill the void, the deep hole the absence of basketball had left.

But I didn't know it then.

I got my first clue from Greg Donaldson. He was living in New York City, doing all the things he had said he was going to do when he'd been at Brown and we had thought it was just another one of his routines. He had a black girlfriend. He hung out with hookers. He took acting lessons. He drove a cab. He taught in an inner-city school. He played pickup basketball on West 4th Street in Greenwich Village, an ongoing outdoor game that's part theater. He called himself an "urbanologist."

"I chase women because it's exciting," he said. "Like a season used to be."

I didn't see the connection at first, thought it was just Donaldson being Donaldson, like when we'd been freshmen and him saying that Coca-Cola ruled the world. It was only later that I came to understand what he was talking about. I had been conditioned to believe life was exciting, for the simple reason that a season was exciting. Basketball always had been a roller coaster of emotion—from game to game, season to season, year to year—turning me into some adrenaline junkie who lived from fix to fix. I had come to believe that life was like that. I had come to expect it, although I certainly didn't know then what "it" was, nor did I understand the reasons I needed it. I had come of age thinking that life was supposed to be exciting, and was now faced with the knowledge that it was not.

Certainly, my job wasn't. Satisfying, yes. Enjoyable, yes. Exciting? No. Nor were relationships exciting. Not after the first rush, anyway. Relationships could be many things, an entire gauntlet of emotions. But exciting? Not really. Not on a daily basis anyway. Not like a season had been. Not in the same way.

So I went from night to night, from relationship to relationship, looking for something, anything, to truly care about, something that would take the place of the game I was so sure I had left behind.

7

"**W**hat do you think of Thoreau?" I asked a beefy kid who sat in the back row, a surly look stamped on his face.

"Thoreau makes me want to throw up," he said.

Another kid would take the cord from the window shades and wrap it around his arm, as though shooting up.

A girl named Mary had a little stick figure on her desk. She called him Milton. Every time she was asked a question she would repeat the question to Milton.

"Milton, what do you think of Thoreau?" Mary would ask.

It was my third year of teaching, the spring of 1972, three years of looking at the same trees outside the window, and I had begun to feel like a magician who had run out of rabbits. Already there was a certain sameness—same script, different students. Already the school had begun to seem claustrophobic, and I knew that if I didn't get out of Barrington High School soon *I* was going to be the one talking to Milton.

I was twenty-six, four years removed from playing basketball, still with no idea of what I wanted to do, other than accumulate experiences the way I once had accumulated points in basketball games.

Henry wanted to go to graduate school, get his Ph.D. He, too, had come to view high-school teaching as a black hole, a role he already had played. He was now divorced, living in a Providence apartment around the corner from me. One night, depressed about the breakup with his wife, he took too many pills. I rushed him to Rhode Island Hospital where his stomach was pumped. He now sat in a wheelchair, looking pale and half dead.

"How do you feel?" the doctor asked.

"What do you care?" Henry snapped, before going into a diatribe about how the country needed socialized medicine. How capitalism didn't care about people, and since the doctor was a member of a capitalist medical system the very idea that he might care for the well-being of one of his patients was ludicrous.

"You can't let those fuckers forget who they really are," he said afterward.

Aaron, married now, had quit teaching. He wanted to work for a newspaper, yet was powerless to actually look for a job. Every morning he got up with his wife who was going off to work, creating the impression he was off job-hunting. The minute she left he went back to sleep. When she returned home in the late afternoon he was watching reruns of TV sitcoms and smoking dope.

"You know those things in the alumni magazine?" he said. "Those ones that say so-and-so is off at graduate school, or

so-and-so has landed a great job, and so-and-so is undoubtedly going to cure cancer in the next year? Just once I'd like
to read where so-and-so 'can't face the world at the present
time.' "

Abe still lived in the small room in his basement, his readings more and more political, readings that kept taking him
farther and farther out on some personal plank.

"I want to be the total teacher," he said. "I don't just
want to teach in a classroom anymore. I want to teach everywhere I go."

I wanted to float, to live forever in the present tense. Things
like having a career, owning your own home, establishing
roots, building a life—they all had become anathema. I lived
in a small apartment near Brown with furniture direct from
the Salvation Army. Everything I owned I could fit in a Car-
man Ghia convertible. I had come to like everything transient,
as though any sense of permanence was some trap I could
never escape from, something to be avoided.

My father had died the spring before, a heart attack at fifty-
six, before we ever had a chance to resolve my resentment
that he had left the family. My mother was remarried, a new
life. My brother, out of the Coast Guard, was married to a
Danish woman and living in Copenhagen. My sister had quit
college after a tortured adolescence. She dressed mostly in
black, lived in an apartment that smelled of incense, and was
afraid to walk to the drugstore at the end of the street, afraid
to go anywhere or do anything other than sit inside and read
Beckett and Sartre and other European intellectuals who
wrote about the meaninglessness of existence. I didn't even
own a basketball anymore. I saw it all as simply another af-
firmation that life was a river, forever moving downhill, taking everything with it. Hadn't *Siddhartha*—or another one of

those silly Herman Hesse novels that were so popular but about as substantial as a chocolate éclair—said that?

Then a funny thing happened.

I went to a basketball game.

A Brown freshman game.

I had been to games before, mostly to check up on the kids who had been freshmen when I was a senior. By this time I was convinced basketball was as far behind me as childhood, as gone as my family and the house we once had lived in on the corner of Bluff Road and Governor Bradford Drive. I had played a handful of times each year, simply for exercise, devoid of any emotional connection, times that convinced me that basketball was just something I used to love.

For the first time, I had friends who didn't know that I once had played basketball, even girlfriends who didn't know and wouldn't have cared. No longer did the game define me, or determine who my friends were. No longer did my life move from game to game. No longer did I think of myself as a player. I read voraciously, going through books like I used to go through sweatsocks.

The Brown freshman team that year was the first predominantly black team in the school's history. Throughout the Ivy League there was a concerted push to attract more minority students. The game plan was for the Ivy schools' minority population to mirror the country's minority population, the result being that almost overnight those schools were dramatically changing.

Basketball teams became an instant beneficiary, many going from all-white to virtually all-black in the course of only a couple of seasons. That certainly was the case at Brown, with a core of kids who arguably would become the best team in the school's history. From the time they arrived, old Marvel

Gym was infused with energy. These kids were a harbinger of the future, young and wild and full of potential. With their large Afros and their ghetto style, they blew through the staid Ivy League like a gust of wind down a dusty hallway.

There was Phil Brown, lean and six foot five, with a fluffy Afro who jumped as if he came off a launching pad. Vaughn Clarke and Lloyd Desvigne. Then there was Eddie Morris, my favorite player, with the biggest Afro of all, a five-foot-ten blur. They were complemented by Jim Busam, a white jump-shooter, but the four black kids were the core, the team's identity. Three of them were from New York City and they brought the city game and all its traditions into Marvel Gym.

From the moment I first saw them I was hooked. From their first game, with their energy and talent and flair, I cared what happened to them. Not in some abstract, intellectual way, the way I felt about so many social causes, but in an intensely personal, emotional way. They gave me something to truly care about.

And I felt a certain guilt about it.

Why was I reacting this way? Why did I care whether a bunch of black kids I didn't know played well or not? Why did I feel such joy in their success? Why did it put me in such a funk when they didn't do well, as if my sense of self had suddenly been transformed to theirs?

Those freshman games became my secret vice.

I drove to New Haven to see Brown play Yale, Don McLean's "American Pie" on the radio. A whole generation lost in space, with no time left to start again. I drove to New Hampshire to watch them play Dartmouth.

The next year it only got worse.

I had quit teaching, convinced I could write a novel. No

matter that I had never written anything more than the quasi-plagiarized gibberish of term papers. Or that I didn't even know how to type. No matter that I possessed none of the skills required to write much of anything, never mind a novel.

The writing had happened quite by accident.

One day in school, having assigned my class some creative writing, and bored by watching them do it, I went to the back of the room and began writing about being a teacher and having nothing to say to a class who had heard it all. Later that night I kept writing, a stream of consciousness that eventually led to about three thousand words, words that all but tumbled over themselves.

Now it was another autumn, one without a job. The novel lay there formless, with no direction, no ending, and no clue how to get to one. I picked apples in the fall, $20 a day, no last name wanted. I did door-to-door surveys in the winter, asking people everything from which commercials they liked to watch, to trying to convince housewives to take me into their kitchens so I could surreptitiously see what canned goods they had. I sold ads for a new weekly local sports paper, until the day I went into a men's store, didn't sell an ad, but bought two shirts, and realized the job was costing me money. I took parts of the novel and tried to sell them to glossy men's magazines as short stories, submissions that eventually would come back dog-eared, with form letters of rejection.

Most of all, I dreamed of going south, of getting away from the New England winter. Or else going to New York and living with Donaldson, who at least was trying to play out his fantasies. Dreamed of going away and starting over—everything I should have done after college, instead of going back to Barrington High School only for the simple reason that it had been easy and available.

Instead, I went to games.

Brown games. Providence College games. University of Rhode Island games. It didn't make any difference anymore. When there were no games to go to, I watched them on television. The games became my sustenance, my small life raft in an ever-turbulent personal sea.

One Saturday afternoon Providence College was playing at two in the Providence Civic Center. At four Brown was playing in Marvel Gym. Then it was off to the University of Connecticut, an hour and a half away, to catch a double-header in the field house on the Storrs campus. Four games in one day, made all the better by having to beat the clock. That was a great day. As was the Big East Tournament held every March, a tournament that began with four games on the opening day, something I looked forward to like a ten-year-old waits for Christmas morning. And it wasn't just watching the four games. It was the feeling at the end of the first game that there were only three left, then two, then one, the feeling that when each game was finished, something irretrievable had been taken away.

I liked to get to the gym early, usually a couple of hours before the game. "Assimilating the arena," I called it. That was the best time: the gym empty, the air heavy with anticipation. Then the gym slowly began to fill up, the beginning of the buzz. It was a little like being a player again, feeling the anxiety rising the closer it got to game time. The feeling that something special was only a little ways away, like the afternoon of a prom.

"Anticipation is greater than realization," Donaldson always had said.

Of course, he was talking about sex.

But the sentiment was the same.

And it was more than just the games. It was the entire sub-culture. The recruiting of players. The endless speculation that concerned the recruiting of players. All the stories and rumors that swirled around the game, the coaching vacancies and who would fill them. This was the romance that surrounded the game, the one I first had been exposed to, reading basket-ball magazines as a kid, and later at basketball camp—this deep unabiding belief that there was a culture that surrounded basketball, one in which the actual games were only the tip of the iceberg.

The new Brown coach was Gerry Alaimo. He had played at Brown in the late 1950s; he had replaced Stan Ward after I graduated. When he arrived at Brown he lived in Marvel Gym for several months. Later, he lived in an apartment a few blocks away, one whose large living room had only a couch, a small chair, a pint-sized TV, and a signed basketball from one of his teams. He was single, and the game consumed him. He was big and gruff, had no social graces, and hated any kind of pretense. But he was loyal and cared about his play-ers, with a heart big as the gym, even if he always tried to dis-guise that fact.

He wore shorts with long white socks throughout the win-ter, wearing long pants only on game days. He hardly ever wore a winter coat, going outside in the dead of winter as if he were some bear. In fact, he called himself "the Big Bruin," Bruins being Brown's team nickname. Shortly into his tenure as the Brown coach he already had turned idiosyncracy into an art form.

"Leave your coat in the car," he said to me one night on the way to a party.

"What do you mean?"

"Just leave your coat in the car, and when I give you the sign get to the car quick," he said, each word sharp and distinct. "Because we're going to be out of there. There will be no time for good-byes."

That's the way it was with him. Turn around and he was gone. Or else he would hang up in the middle of a phone conversation. No good-byes.

We had many similarities. We both had played for Stan Ward. We both had used basketball to get into Brown, both had passed through the school as outsiders, basketball as the lifeline. We both had an aversion to a lot of social graces and pretense. And, of course, we both liked games.

We often would go together, either to scout some future Brown opponent, or check out some prospective recruit who was within driving distance. The ritual was always the same. He drove his car to the game. I drove his car home, during which ride he would take the orange cooler out of the trunk and begin downing beers, one after another, the first one disappearing in three or four large swallows. Then he searched for scores on the radio, or else some game to listen to.

Through him, I got closer to the subculture, the cult world of assistant coaches, summer camps, clinics, the part of college basketball that the average fan had little access to. Being a former player gave me a certain credibility, like men who once had been to war together. But it was more than that. I went to games with Alaimo and his assistants, sat at the press table, and liked being an insider, liked knowing things that others didn't. Liked the fact that if anyone mentioned a town in New England I could almost always name a player who had come from there. It was like being back at basketball camp again, part of some network, some fraternity with its secret handshakes and private rules. A life could be lived within these parameters, a life that made sense.

Once again, basketball was starting to determine who my friends were, as it had done during my childhood.

I went to the games early in the evening, then to parties later. Parties where most of the people considered sports to be a microcosm of everything wrong with America: competitive, male-oriented, obsessed with winning. In short, an embodiment of the same mentality that now had us stuck in Vietnam. And while I certainly knew it was infinitely more complicated than that, I went along with the same analysis, believing that at some fundamental level I had been scarred by basketball.

But I still loved the games.

They were more than an escape. They were some link to something I didn't understand, something at the very core of what I had become.

So it began.

Soon the games began to take on their own reality, exempt from anything else that surrounded them. I planned my day around them, looked toward them in anticipation. They became the daily treat, something to savor. I awoke on game day feeling the day was special, the upcoming game a light at the end of some tunnel, something that had nothing to do with the high school or teaching or any of the things I considered my real life.

Not that I saw it as a problem.

The games are just something to do, I told myself, certainly not something to be concerned about. *Basketball is still a game I've outgrown,* I told myself. *This team is simply an aberration.* Still, once again a basketball season was defining what I did. Dates were juggled around games, or else broken.

Excuses were made. One weekend I picked up Nancy in Boston. She had been my girlfriend for about a year, was now a senior at Boston University. She shared many of the leftist leanings I did, but she was going to be a nurse and had the kind of focus about the future and her place in it that I still lacked. It was February, a rare weekend devoid of home games. The plan was to go to Cape Cod, a get-away weekend. I was even looking forward to it, convinced that it would be a good chance to clear my head, away from the games.

Yet on the drive to the Cape, going down Route 3 on one of those bright, sunny February afternoons, I suddenly realized North Carolina was playing Maryland on television, a big game at the time. It was a Maryland team that featured Tom McMillen and John Lucas, a showcase team playing a showcase game, and not being able to watch it was like going cold turkey. It was all I could do to keep driving the car. Everything Nancy said, no matter how trivial, made me irritable. I knew it was irrational, knew I was acting like an idiot, but the very thought of not being able to watch the game was making me crazy. I looked at the clock on the dashboard, thinking that it would probably be halftime by now, an hour into the game. The next hour was near torture, a feeling of incredible deprivation. Only when I figured the game was over did I start to relax.

I would undergo the same scenario many times in the years afterward. Those times when I would do something else rather than go to the game, the game was constantly on my mind. The evening became all about looking at the clock, wondering what point in the game it was, wondering what was happening, like some high-school wallflower sitting home fantasizing about the elaborate party going on down the street.

But I never talked about this with Nancy, never talked about it with anyone.

It was still a secret vice, something hidden from my friends, all the ones I knew would never understand, who'd see it as some manifestation that I must have been kidnapped by aliens and brainwashed. You couldn't have a political consciousness and be a basketball fan too.

"Why are these damn games so important?" Nancy asked. "I don't understand it."

"Hey, some people drink, some people gamble, some people go to games. Isn't that what America's all about? The opportunity to have the vice of your choice?"

"I'm serious," she said.

"I don't know," I said. "I just like them."

"That's not good enough," she countered. "It's more than that—more than you just like them. It's like something happens to you. Something comes over you and you become a different person. Someone I don't even like."

Not surprising. Nancy wanted a normal relationship, not spending a Saturday evening in some old gym watching a college basketball game, then going out later and talking about it. She wanted a future that didn't include basketball games in it.

Eventually, the games became a metaphor for everything that went wrong with me in relationships with women. Women wanted commitment, the promise of permanence. I wanted to go to games. Women wanted some shared experience, I got most of my satisfaction from something that excluded them. Women wanted some vision of the future, something we both would share. I couldn't see beyond the next game.

Nor was I honest about it. I had long since developed an

ability to deceive, to put a positive spin on things. Little wonder. Hadn't I been deceiving myself for years? Wasn't I forever putting a positive spin on my own behavior by refusing to confront the reasons for it? I was attracted to women who tended to be vaguely leftish and countercultural, women who viewed sports as just one more manifestation of the mainstream culture that they denigrated. Women who would have avoided any man who was a sports freak as if he had leprosy. So in the beginning, I would hide the games from them.

"I'm not really a sports fan," I would say. "I just like basketball."

I even half believed it. I made fun of the men who sat in front of the television on Sunday afternoons and watched professional football, as if I were somehow morally superior because I wasn't infatuated with the NFL, or didn't faithfully follow baseball. I had little patience with the guys who talked of their golf games, viewing golf as little more than Republican religion, too many memories of caddying as a kid. I made fun of all the guys who played in softball leagues, with their expensive uniforms and their endless tournaments, in a rather obvious attempt to recapture some lost youth. As if my obsession was somehow more noble than theirs, some magnificent quest.

The pattern was always the same. Eventually there would be a new girlfriend and a private vow that this time was going to be different. No more seasons. No more games. I still was naive enough to think I could control it, that going to games was simply a choice, like going to the movies.

But I couldn't control it. Or at least, I wouldn't.

Like the time Brown was in contention for the Ivy League title, faced with Penn and Princeton on the road, their annual dream-killer of a trip. *I'm not going to go,* I told myself. *Not this time. Enough of these odyssey weekends.* Instead, I was going to go by train to Baltimore to see a friend, the first weekend in a while with no games in it. But when the train pulled into Philadelphia's 30th Street Station it was shortly before 7 P.M., when Brown was scheduled to play Penn in the Palestra just a few blocks away. At the last instant I left the train and went up the stairs into the crowded station.

"How do I get to the Palestra?" I asked the guy in the information booth.

"Go up two blocks to Walnut Street and take a left," he said. "It's down there somewhere."

It was a couple of minutes after seven. Outside the station the roads were coated with snow, the air full of sleet. I put my suitcase in my right hand and started running.

I went two blocks and all I saw was a big warehouse. No Walnut Street. No University of Pennsylvania. Nothing. I ran across a railroad bridge, alternately changing hands carrying the suitcase. Finally I saw Franklin Field off in the distance, shrouded in darkness. I knew the Palestra was next door.

When I finally got inside Brown was leading, and I thought about the first time I ever saw the Palestra. It was 1966, my sophomore year, back when the Palestra was one of the college game's sacred temples. There were nine thousand lunatics in the stands. The only problem was they all were waiting for LaSalle and Villanova in the second game. Penn was blowing us out that night and the boisterous crowd spent the last ten minutes of the game alternately cheering for the next game and throwing paper airplanes at us.

The old gym still looked the same: wooden bleachers, large banners. Listen carefully and you could hear the echoes of yesterday's cheers, feel the presence of all the ghosts, the innumerable players who had played on the varnished court. I sat high up in the bleachers behind one of the baskets, my suitcase next to me. I was glad I was there, even if I already had missed the next train to Baltimore. The last one was at 8:49.

With a couple of minutes left, Brown leading in a close game, I stood in an end-zone ramp, trying to get one last peek. It was 8:35, getting close. A few minutes later I bolted, running back through the snow-covered streets, feeling as exhausted as if I had played, just making the train as it pulled out of the station heading south.

The next day my friend and I were on the way out to Washington. The plan was to get together with some of her friends in Georgetown, but the closer we got the more I wanted to be at the Brown game at Princeton. You can go out for dinner in Georgetown anytime, right?

"You can't be serious." she said.

A few minutes later we turned around and started heading for Princeton, New Jersey. It was four-thirty.

"How far away is it?" she asked.

"Not that far," I lied. "A couple of hours."

Three hours later we were lost in a Trenton ghetto, she had stopped talking, and I was feeling guilty.

"Okay," I finally said. "It was a stupid idea. I feel bad I got you lost in Trenton on a Saturday night."

"Don't feel sorry about that," she said. "I'd rather be lost in Trenton than watching a stupid basketball game."

We eventually found Jadwyn Gym, arriving at halftime. Brown was losing, and continued to lose in the second half.

"Was it worth it?" she asked.

"Sure," I said.

She said she didn't understand.

Not that she should. After all, no one ever threw paper airplanes at her in the Palestra.

Every summer there would be a certain decompression, along with a personal pep talk. *No more,* I'd tell myself. *Next year is going to be different.* I would make a plan to get out of Rhode Island for the winter, go somewhere and take the novel out of the drawer. Go someplace and get all those wanderlust fantasies out of my head once and for all. At such times I wished I could be more like my brother who had left both Barrington and Rhode Island far behind him, who had traveled extensively around the world, who had so obviously moved on to a new phase in his life.

But then would come another fall, the leaves beginning to change, the basketball magazines on the newsstands, the eve of another season, and I would start to get hooked all over again. As if nothing had really changed since I was twelve years old and trying out for the junior-high team.

And eventually the new girlfriend would realize what the old ones had come to know: that she couldn't really compete with the games. That if and when it finally came down to a choice—her or the games—I was going to choose the games.

"Are you disillusioned?" Libby asked.

I looked across the table at her at a restaurant in Harvard Square in Cambridge. She was young and hopeful, her life all ahead of her. She was still in college, talked of going to Europe, her dreams as big as the ocean. She had been raised on the top of a Vermont mountain across the river from Dartmouth, often had gone to school by skiing down the mountain. She also had grown up with reclusive writer J. D. Salinger's children, and had a love of books that equaled my own.

Disillusioned?

Where to begin? With the novel that was little more than a pipe dream? With a succession of nowhere jobs? With calling myself a "freelance writer," a euphemism for being unemployed? Where to begin?

She was a student at the University of New Hampshire and often I would go there to visit her. The school was in Durham, a wonderful little college town with student bars and restaurants and one movie theater. It all seemed idyllic, the quaintness of the town, the beauty of the campus, a college direct from the pages of a recruitment brochure. Libby loved her courses, knew several of her professors personally, was a serious student. She talked of courses and books, of ideas. This was the college experience I had missed, college the way it was supposed to have been, instead of always going to the gym, living from season to season, basketball as a full-time job. Such visits only reinforced for me how crippling the game had been, the price I had paid for it. During those times in Durham, I could envision a life without games, a life that would be somehow purer.

Right from the beginning Libby made it clear she had no interest in games. All around her in the Providence Civic Center people would be cheering and yelling at the refs, all the tumult of a college basketball game in a large sold-out arena of thirteen thousand people, and she would be reading Doris Lessing or Margaret Atwood, some feminist who wrote about a world very different than the Providence Civic Center. Libby's strategy was simple: Ignore the games and perhaps they would go away.

They didn't.

One afternoon we were at a ski chalet in New Hampshire, another one of those rare winter weekends away from a game.

But now it was four in the afternoon, Brown was playing at Harvard that night, and if we left right now we could get to Cambridge by eight, and this was a big game, a really important game, and if she did this favor for me I would do two for her, and on and on it went, a conversation that always made me feel like a method actor in a long-running play, the words on remote control.

"Come on," I all but pleaded. "It will be fun. We'll talk all the way. No radio. We'll talk all the way, go out to eat in Cambridge after, and we'll be back by two. Think of it as an adventure."

"All right," she finally consented.

So we drove the three hours to Cambridge, arriving just in time, climbed the four flights of the stairs to Harvard's old gym, the one I used to play in. I cradled my anticipation, she her book. It was a Harvard team of James Brown, the man who eventually would go on to become a network sports commentator. He had been one of the elite high-school players in the country at DeMatha, the famed basketball school on the outskirts of Washington, D.C., supposedly recruited to Harvard by Teddy Kennedy. I liked knowing all that; it was like looking at a game the way archaeologists supposedly look at ruins, down through the layers. I didn't just watch a game. I had to know where the players came from, where they had gone to high school, as much about them as I could.

Afterward, we began driving the three hours back, through New Hampshire on the lonely interstate in the wee hours of the morning. It was cold and dark outside, a New England winter.

"Can you explain it to me? I mean really explain it to me?" Libby said. "Because you never do. You talk around it, and you make jokes about it, but you never really explain it.

I used to think it was that you simply don't want to grow up, but I know it's not that simple. But I still can't understand it. It's so foreign to me. And if anyone had ever told me that I would be involved with someone whose idea of a big night out is going to a basketball game, I never would have believed it."

The silence hung between us in the darkened car. How to explain that the games had become the only thing that made me feel truly alive? The only thing that took me out of myself, took me to some exalted personal place, away from problems and bills? How to explain that being a player was the only dream I had ever had, and that dream had ended when I was twenty-three years old? How to explain that shooting a basketball was the thing I did best in all the world, a skill that now had no value, worthless as a childhood toy? How to explain to her that I now lived for the games for reasons that I could barely understand, never mind articulate—that everything else was filler, the things I did to pass the time before the games started.

"They are the one constant in my life," I finally said. "Everything else has changed. My family has changed. My friends have changed. Everything changes. But the games don't. When I go to the game it's timeless. I relate to it the same way I did when I was ten years old. It's the only thing that hasn't changed. Does that make any sense?"

Not to her it didn't.

But there were others who shared my obsession.

One was Jimmy Cox, who always seemed to be hanging around Brown basketball games, part of the scene. He had led the state in scoring while playing for a Providence high school, graduating two years ahead of me. He then had gone to Providence College, one of the small handful of Rhode Island kids to be recruited by PC, his fate to play behind Jimmy Walker.

He had grown up near Brown, had come of age sneaking into Marvel Gym, just another kid sneaking in shooting on one of the side baskets until Stan Ward threw him out.

"I've been thrown out in three decades now," he said.

A few years before, he used to hang around our parties at Brown, although he rarely participated. He didn't drink, rarely swore, avoided the bacchanalia that the rest of us often indulged in. He was the ultimate observer. He was religious in way that the rest of us weren't anymore, and one night, leaving a fraternity party in the early hours of the morning, people drunk, couples making out, the detritus of the evening visible everywhere, he turned and said, with a shake of his head, "If there's no Heaven I'm screwed."

We talked about basketball constantly. About teams and players. About strategies. About who could coach and who couldn't. The game was the spine of our friendship, provided a shared way of looking at the world, just as it had done with my childhood friends.

Cox was the first person I knew who looked at basketball intellectually. He didn't just watch games, he studied them, critiqued them. He charted teams, gave them power ratings long before it became fashionable. He wanted to know why teams won. He was a teacher-coach in a Rhode Island city south of Providence, but was frustrated by it.

"It's not the big time," he said, reading off a litany of woes, everything from the bus rides to the goofy kids with their bell-bottoms to the sense that no one cared about high-school basketball anymore. "It's the minitime."

Cox flirted with the idea of trying to get into college coaching, something closer to that elusive "big time" that hung out in the distance like a mountain in the mist. Like me, though, he was torn between his love for the game and his desire not to let it define him. He wanted no part of working at the innumerable summer basketball camps that had become the breeding ground of assistant coaches, was not suited for the ass-kissing and politics that so often went into who got the jobs and who didn't. Cox was a purist in an impure world, and that realization made him the ultimate cynic, a detached critic, both of basketball and the world around him.

We were alike in that sense, too.

We went to the beach in the summer and talked about basketball, the upcoming season. We went to summer league games together. We drove to St. John's in New York to watch Providence College play an NCAA playoff game, down and back in the same day, getting back long after midnight. We did the same thing to watch Brown play Manhattan in Madison Square Garden, then woke up after only a couple of hours' sleep to teach the next day. I lived in two different worlds that had little to do with one another.

Every June we went to the "Boston Shootout," one of the first showcase high-school all-star games, the best players from several different cities. In those early years it was an almost exclusively black event, the players, the fans, the ambience. It was like looking at the game's future, and I felt privileged to be a part of it, right there with the coaches and the people for whom the game was their life. We saw players there who went on to be big college stars, ones who went on to be pros; we felt like talent scouts, there at the creation.

Cox and I drove to St. Louis together in 1973 to watch Providence College play in the Final Four. It was my first Final Four, a visit to the college basketball mecca, with scores of famous coaches milling around. This was the college game's biggest stage; there was the sense that you were watching basketball history.

Four years later I went again, driving all the way from Providence to Atlanta even though I didn't have a ticket. On the way I stopped in North Carolina because I figured you couldn't be a true basketball fan unless you had seen both the University of North Carolina in Chapel Hill and Duke in Durham. The game's famous schools, the famous gyms, they were the sacred shrines to me. Not museums. Not theaters. Gyms.

On the way to Atlanta I thought about when I'd seen Madison Square Garden for the first time. That was the old Garden, the one on Eighth Avenue, complete with the marquee that hung out over the sidewalk and the gamblers in the corners of the lobby talking out of the sides of their mouths. It was all incredibly romantic. Raffa, Joey DeSisto, Pat Monti, and myself had taken the train from Providence to New York, my first real trip. We all stayed in one room in a fleabag hotel near the Garden, ate in cafeterias, went to a porno theater in the afternoon. A rube's tour.

After the game we had gone looking for girls. We would have had a better chance trying to find King Solomon's mines. Eventually, we saw a sign that said, Dance with Girls. How were we supposed to know that it cost money?

"This city sucks," Raffa had said. "Two bucks for a hamburger. There should be a law."

But I had loved it, even though our New York journey had nothing to do with Rockefeller Center, the Statue of Liberty, or any of the other tourist attractions, and was basically confined to about three blocks. New York to me was Madison Square Garden. Anything else was a postcard.

Road trips to games always had been part of being a player.

In high school we'd traveled to the old New England Tournament in the Boston Garden, right there on the same parquet floor where the Celtics played. We would drive up there and watch four games in a row, all those schools whose names resonated with basketball legend in New England: Hillhouse and Wilbur Cross in New Haven; Hartford Public, with the great Eddie "Pumpkin" Griffin, one of New England's first great black high-school stars; Cambridge Rindge and Latin. Or else it was going to the old Rhode Island Auditorium in Providence to see the Celtics play, six guys in Normie Fiedler's car, radio up, heater on to ward off the New England winter.

There was nothing I liked better in those days than going to games. It was better than parties, better than dates, better than driving around town. Those were magical times, the sense that the game was some large force that you could hook into, something much bigger than yourself, but you could be a part of it too.

So driving to Atlanta was just another chapter, albeit a current one.

It was still a few years before the Final Four became the mega–media event it is now, and I spent time at the coaches' convention. I went to the lectures, hung around the lobby of the Hyatt, even went to the coaches' interviews. The hot coach that year was Marquette's Al McGuire, and I was mesmerized by him, by his idiosyncacies, his New York expressions, like calling fancy play "French pastry." That was the year McGuire won, and as the clock wound down, McGuire cried on the bench. Afterward he said that he was thinking of all the little gyms he'd been in, all the little gyms with the small lockers and the cold-water showers, the long journey that had taken him to the national championship. I related to all of that. Just being at the Final Four, being a part of the proceedings in a small way, made me feel more connected to basketball.

On Saturday afternoon, the day of the national semifinal double-header, I bought a ticket from a scalper. His name was Rodney Parker, and he had been featured in a wonderful book about New York City basketball called *Heaven Is a Playground*. In the book he'd been described as a glorified street agent, someone who helped kids in a Brooklyn neighborhood into various colleges, but made his money scalping tickets.

"Did you read the book?" I asked Parker.

"Just the parts about myself," he said.

Al McGuire and Rodney Parker. To me, it was Basketball Heaven.

Yet I resisted writing about sports.

To write about them would have been an admission that I hadn't put them behind me, that I was still essentially one-dimensional, that nothing had changed. And I so wanted things to have changed.

I told myself continuously that they had. I read more books, went to more movies, had more conversations that had nothing to do with basketball. I did articles on a wide variety of subjects, knew that writing was a skill, and I was getting better at it. Yet the reality was that it was more and more difficult to eke out even a meager living at it, since freelancing locally is the lowest rung of journalism. So I wrote some advertising copy. I did some business projects. I tried to hustle more, anything to keep the wolf from the door.

"Why not be a sports writer?" Raffa said. "It would be a joke. Go to games and write about them. For someone like you that would be a joke."

No way, I would say.

Sports belonged to the past, right? Right there with Dinah and the house in Barrington, and memories of a family that had become uprooted.

Then there would be a game that night and I would look forward to it all day.

And there was something comforting about knowing that all my college friends still followed the game, that sports still were our common denominator. It was the knowledge that if there was a big game on television, whether it was college or the NBA, virtually everyone I had ever known was watching it. Donaldson and Landau in New York. Sarles in Providence. Sigur in Atlanta. Raffa in Barrington. Everyone.

Games were still the things that connected us, that and our shared history. Games and players were our reference points, the way we instantly caught up with each other. Somehow it didn't matter that the years were passing and our lives were going in different directions; the games were the one connector.

Raffa was still teaching and coaching. He had three kids by now, still lived in Barrington, but basketball was beginning to get in the way.

"She resents it," he said of his wife Linda, whom he referred to as "the Big L." "She resents all the time it takes."

We were watching an NBA playoff game on television in his house, something we did a lot. He had been married for about seven years, approaching that time in a marriage when there are few illusions left, reality having settled in. His wife wanted a bigger house, a better car, more of the things that were supposed to go with living in Barrington, the traditional measuring-sticks of success. Raffa simply wanted to raise his kids and coach his team.

"She thinks she has to compete with basketball," he said.

"What's her problem?" I asked. "She knew you wanted to coach."

"Tell 'the Big L' that," he said.

When they first had gotten married Linda had gone to his games, the loyal wife. No more.

Then again, he had been the one who always said you should never bring a girl to an athletic event.

Sarles was now working in a Providence bank, rapidly rising through the ranks. He had played only a year and a half of college basketball, but when he quit, it had been a national story, right there on the Associated Press wire. He had been the captain of the Amherst team while only a sophomore, when the coach discovered two guys on the team had been drinking in season, a team violation. One of them was the actor Ken Howard, who later would become "the White Shadow" of television fame. So the coach threw the two off the team. At which point Sarles objected, essentially saying that everyone on the team drank and if the coach was going to throw those two off, he should throw Sarles off too. So the coach did. I remember seeing the story in the paper and smiling to myself. It seemed so much like Jay: principled, no bullshit.

After Amherst, he had gone to law school at Stanford. During his first year there, UCLA, with Lew Alcindor, was the best college team in the country. Sarles had stood in line for hours to get a ticket to see them when they came to play Stanford. On the day of the game Alcindor was sick, didn't play. Sarles was so upset that he got into his car, quit law school, and drove the three thousand miles home.

Occasionally, we would bump into each other at Providence College games. He was still a big basketball fan, yet not a fanatic. He seemingly had had little trouble moving beyond the game. Then again, he always had been so grounded, so focused. He always possessed a game plan for his life, a vision of a future beyond basketball that I had never seen.

Sometimes I would take trips with the Brown basketball team, brought along by Gerry Alaimo. It was a way of feeling a part of a team again, if only an illusory experience. The long bus ride. The hotel. The game in some different gym. The locker room. Caring who won. Dissecting it afterward, taking a forty-minute game and analyzing it as if it were some lab specimen under a microscope. It was like being a player again, the closest I could get.

Yet I still clung to the illusion that this was just some aberrant part of my life, the belief that my real life was teaching and books, grand ideas and the accumulation of experiences, that I had moved far beyond the sports of my youth. That this momentary little obsession with games was merely temporary, some inexplicable flight of fancy, and it certainly had nothing to do with my real life.

One night, coming back from the Penn-Princeton trip, I sat by the window in a darkened bus late at night, looking out the window, just as I had done in February of 1968, the night I started resenting my childhood obsession with the game. The irony was inescapable. So many things had happened, yet nothing had. Once again I was riding in a darkened bus late at night, coming back from some losing road trip, wondering what I was doing.

But by the mid-1970s, with no real job and dwindling money, the games had become all I had.

8

knew my life no longer worked the day the sheriff knocked on my door with a summons to appear in court for an overextended credit card loan.

I was thirty-three, had been out of college ten years, and had no money. My car, nearly a decade old, was constantly breaking down. It seemed a symbol of my life. I was behind in the rent. I needed new glasses, but couldn't afford to go to the eye doctor. Every time I watched television all I could focus on was the sports jacket someone was wearing and the chilling realization that I couldn't afford it. I lived from freelance check to freelance check, always behind, with no real hope of ever getting ahead, caught in some economic maze from which there seemed no exit. The lack of money was coloring everything, like looking at the world through gray gauze.

I spent too many nights in bars, too many nights drinking vodka and grapefruit juice, too many nights telling the same

stories to different women, too many mornings waking up in
some unfamiliar place with a throbbing headache and matching guilt.

It was the late 1970s, a sexual salad bar. No herpes. No
AIDS. No obvious price tag for a sybaritic lifestyle. A singles-
bar culture had sprung up in Providence and we were right in
the middle of it: Eddie Shein, who had gone to Brown a couple of years ahead of me, and believed in what he called "sex
and dismissal." Bob Woods, a year behind me in high school.
And Walter Hackett, who called himself "the Stroker," from
his old tennis-playing days. He was ten years older than me,
already had gone from idiosyncratic to eccentric.

The first night I met Hackett he was sitting in a Providence
bar with several women, telling them he once had played
freshman football at Northwestern, had taught freshman English at Brown, had worked in the fashion industry in New
York, and now was working on the Great American Novel.
All this in an accent that kept getting more affected as the
evening wore on. All the while he was ordering drinks for the
table with a flourish, telling the waitress to put it on his personal tab, and eventually telling the women that if they
weren't so Providence Provincial they could come back to the
town house with him and explore "existential nothingness."

Shortly afterward, the women having left and the evening
grown late, he threw his yellow sweater with the little alliga-
tor on it over his shoulder, got into the old white Cadillac
convertible with the top down, screamed, "EEEH . . . AHH!"
into the night and drove off.

A few minutes later he drove his car into a bridge abutment,
narrowly avoiding injury.

"The Stroker." What better nickname for an itinerant
teaching tennis pro?

"I got the forehand blues," he sang, whenever he got the chance. *"Just stroking my life away."*

That, too, was fitting. In Hackett's view of the universe all the frailties of the human condition came down to the fact that he couldn't hit a tennis forehand. As if that had somehow become symbolic of his life, the one tragic flaw. He was forever moving his right hand across his body in a simulated tennis stroke, as though in search of the perfect forehand. Not that he really dwelled on it. To the Stroker, life was a cabaret, old chum, an ongoing party. He had grown up in an age where you played hard and partied harder, and from an early age he had turned it into an art form. He had a bundleful of one-liners, complete with a self-deprecating humor, and in a stuffy, white bread, uptight world, he was an antidote. He was irreverent, profane, vulgar, often in incredibly bad taste, sometimes all at once. But he always made me laugh, a not insignificant gift in a country that was poised to enter the Reagan years.

And there wasn't any town house. Just as there never had been any freshman football at Northwestern or teaching freshman English at Brown. There was no Great American Novel in the draw. He had grown up in a tenement over a bar. Both his parents had been alcoholics. He hadn't gone to college. In a sense he was a little like James Gatz, the poor midwestern kid who transformed himself into the urbane Jay Gatsby, with his silk shirts and his big dreams. The Stroker was like that, making it up as he went along, seduced by the "Waspy" tennis world he was so attracted to. He said he knew five minutes of everything, just enough to get by at cocktail parties, just enough to con people.

Once he had lived off several women, relying on his tennis ability and a certain charm. Now—older, too heavy, the little money he once had gone as childhood summers—he lived in one small room. He always seemed to wear the same yellow sweater, one that often reeked with body odor. He gave tennis lessons whenever he could find a spare court. Often, too tired and hungover to actually hit balls with the people he was teaching, he would give some kid a couple of bucks to do it for him, while he sat under a tree in a Panama hat sipping vodka out of a tennis-ball can. Once he had been one of the best tennis players in the state. Now it was all memories and old stories.

Many summer nights he showed up outside my apartment, top down on the convertible, show tunes coming out of the radio, singing, *"What are the simple joys of maidenhood?"* at two in the morning. *"Life is a cabaret, old chum,"* whether you want it to be or not.

Friday was our big night out. I sat on a couch in the late afternoons in the Rusty Scupper restaurant in Providence, looking out the bay windows over the city, waiting for happy hour to start, full of anticipation of the evening, the promise of possibilities. Like waiting for a game to start, the quiet before the explosion. Existential evenings, I called them, evenings that could wind up anywhere.

Hackett always started off with some double scotches, his warm-up drink. A few of those and it was on to martinis, hours of them, until you looked at him and wondered how any human being could drink this much and still be vertical. Invariably, this would be followed by a declaration of Wild Turkey, the drink he later described as making you feel like you had a dozen rats running up your leg. The evolution of the drinks mirrored the evolution of his performance. Early in the evening he was charming, funny, the life of the party. Then he would get louder, more vulgar, on his way to being a social leper.

"To quote Lawrence Durrell in the Alexandria Quartet," he

said to two women one night. "Life is like a cucumber. In your left hand one minute, up your ass the next."

"Lawrence who?" one of the women asked. "The Alexander what?"

"Remember one thing, ladies," Hackett said. "Who is short and who is tall. And who is to say who is short and who is tall?"

With the advent of the Wild Turkey came the werewolf times. The mean edge. Out of control. Off in some private place where his demons all were out of their cages. Like the time at a beach bar when Hackett ended up on a stage wearing a gray helmet, billing himself as the "pope of punk rock" and singing "The Forehand Blues" as people lobbed ashtrays at him.

Or the time we were in one of those sing-along restaurants. Hackett liked those, for he fancied himself an entertainer. The singer, who was doing mostly Irish songs, was looking for willing participants. At first, he considered Hackett an ally, continually playing to him, always looking at our table as he sang. But as the evening wore on, the singer, now realizing that Hackett already had crossed the line from jovial customer to drunken pariah, tried to ignore him. Which was a mistake with the Stroker, who demanded to be the center of attention.

"Sing 'Danny Boy,' " Hackett yelled.

The singer tried to ignore him.

"Sing 'Danny Boy'!" Hackett yelled again.

Again, the singer ignored him.

"*Sing 'Danny Boy'!*" Hackett yelled, louder this time, standing up, everyone in the room now looking at him.

Again, the singer ignored him, tried to pretend that this large man, now out of his seat commanding everyone's attention, was going to go away.

No such luck.

"Sing 'Danny Boy,' you Irish cocksucker!" Hackett screamed.

But he was never better than at the dinner parties that we would occasionally get invited to, although how we did now defies logic. Hackett cut through all pretense. One night, we went to a Providence party where there were several academics from Brown. It was being hosted by a red-haired woman named Barbara, who told Shein that she thought "the Stroker" was really kind of charming in an American Primitive kind of way. Hackett called her "Major Barbara," and started asking her if she wanted to go upstairs and do a *"Fantasy Island"* thing, at which point Barbara said she had to check on the fondue. It was the time when feminism was in bloom, and you couldn't go to an East Side cocktail party without the conversation eventually turning to how oppressive white males were. This night it was Hemingway. How all his books should be burned, or banned, or some such thing.

Hackett had come into the room, deep into the Wild Turkey, looking at the people.

"You can talk all you want about Hemingway and what a sexist he was," he said dramatically, lapsing once again into a fake British accent. "You can talk all you want about his imagery and his inherent messages, and you can pretend that you know everything about him. But remember one thing."

He paused for effect. Hackett always was pausing for effect.

"I'm the only person in this room who once blew him."

Eventually it was apparent that all his self-destructive behavior, his prodigious drinking, were starting to take their toll on Hackett. There had been too many bridges burned. Too many late nights. Too many days on a cycle of late-night drinking followed by sleeping until noon.

Shein tried to help him. Shein was slender and dark-haired, had known him for years through tennis. Shein was an art dealer, moved skillfully through both the world of New York galleries and Providence singles bars. He even once had been a guest on *The Tonight Show,* thanks to his finding some paintings by three eighteenth-century black artists and resurrecting their reputations, and to a business relationship he had with Bill Cosby, who had guest-hosted the program that night.

"Hackett's funnier," Shein said of Cosby.

Shein continually gave Hackett odd jobs to do, ways to give Hackett money, and remained his benefactor.

"The train leaves right now, Hackett," Shein said one night, "and you either get on it, or you walk forever. There's no other choice. What's it going to be? Either get on the train or walk forever."

"I'll hitchhike," Hackett said defiantly.

Hitchhike he did. Often with me alongside.

Lying in bed at ten in the morning after some blurry nightbefore, there was a story on the radio about long lines at the malls for Christmas shopping, and how there had been traffic problems in the commuter rush hour. *I do none of it,* I thought. And it wasn't even by design anymore, but simply by the way things had evolved. There was no job to get up in the morning for, no early-morning traffic to fight through. No money for Christmas presents. No food in the refrigerator. No career. More and more I was on the fringe of society, drifting off in the margins. I still lived from freelance story to freelance story, but there was no more romance to it. Once, money had meant virtually nothing to me, so convinced was I that I'd rejected the bourgeois values of my childhood. Now the lack of it meant everything.

The sixties that had shaped me were not long over, but it was as if they never happened. Disco poured out of sound systems in clubs like some bad perversion of the rock music that once was supposed to have been on the cutting edge, the anthems of a generation that was going to change the country. Guys who used to rail against materialism were now driving BMWs, the "Me Decade" in all its finery. Once business suits had been seen as the symbols of male oppression, and makeup the symbol of female oppression. Now they were the epitome of style.

Even sports had made a big comeback.

No longer did you hear talk of sports being a manifestation of all the evils of society. Or that athletes all were symbols of some pervasive establishment. Or that they all were conservative politically, defenders of the past. Those sentiments seemed dated, as obsolete as two-handed set shots in basketball. Sports were the new religion, with more games on television, bigger salaries for players, bigger crowds, more interest.

This was all correlated with the rise of the fitness industry, and the growing awareness that being in shape was a lifetime thing, not merely something that ended when you became an adult. People who never played a sport in their lives as kids were now walking around in warm-up suits. America was starting to look like a country where everyone was on the way to the gym.

It was a different America than it had been just a few years before, one in which money and possessions were the new gods, a society genuflecting in front of them. I had neither.

The writing was going better, though. I sold articles continuously, to all sorts of low-paying publications, many to the Sunday magazine of the Providence *Journal*. Almost anything except sports. I didn't want to write sports. Sports were behind me, right? I fancied myself as a real writer, ready to tackle the big issues of the culture and try to make some sense out of them. Freelancing was wonderful, provided access to all sorts of interesting people and places, and I knew I was getting better at it, bringing to it much of the same dedication I once had brought to being a player. I struggled over articles, worked at getting better, convinced that writing was a skill that you could improve, just like shooting baskets.

Doing articles also was a substitute for playing basketball, a certain sublimation, even if I didn't realize it at the time. It gave me something to get excited about, feel passionate about.

It just didn't pay enough.

So I drifted from story to story, forever waiting for the next check, never having enough money. Careers were for other people. I was trying to survive. And all the while my life was getting more out of control.

I had never been much of a drinker, even in college. Never was one to sit at home and drink alone. But more and more I had drifted into some dark season, a nightlife that revolved around bars and clubs, seduced by the energy, the escape, the promise of possibilities. In retrospect, the clubs had become a substitute for the excitement playing had given me, although I didn't realize it then. But more and more there were hangover mornings, times I woke up and wanted to blot out the night before, like a bad game you wanted to see disappear. Not that I ever really saw the drinking as a problem. I always remembered what I had done the night before, however embarrassing, always remembered what I had said, however stupid or ill-advised. I convinced myself that I was just a social drinker, could stop anytime I wanted.

Until the morning I woke up in a strange room with an incredible headache. There were two young kids in the room going through the drawers in a dresser across the room.

"We're looking for eggs," one of them said.

"Eggs?"

"Easter eggs."

I pulled the covers up over my head, trying to blot this all out. Where was I? What had happened the night before? All I remembered were a couple of bars, too many vodkas, and too many stupid conversations.

Suddenly a woman I knew from the clubs walked into the room. I didn't know her very well, didn't know where she lived, or even that she had kids.

"I'm sorry about the kids," she said. "I didn't know they were in here."

She looked at me closely.

"Are you all right?"

"I'm a little hurtin'," I said. "What happened?"

"You kind of fell asleep right before last call, and we didn't think you should drive, so I brought you home. You don't remember? Nothing happened."

I held my throbbing head in my hands, thanked her.

She seemed as embarrassed as I was.

"We'll be going to church in a while and I'll drop you off at the club."

An hour later I sat in the front seat in my rumpled clothes. The woman was dressed up. The two kids in their Easter best sat in the backseat. I wanted to disappear in a puff of smoke. *Never again,* I told myself. *Never, never again.*

"Thank you," I said, when she dropped me off at my car.

"Happy Easter," said one of the kids.

It was the worst hangover of my life, one that kept me in bed for the rest of the day, complete with a vow never to drink that way again, a vow that's been kept ever since. I had had a million laughs, but then it felt like a party feels at three in the morning when everyone's gone home and all that's left are the empty cups on the floor and smell of stale beer.

With that hangover came the chilling realization that I had been deceiving myself. For a couple of years I had been comparing myself to the Stroker and feeling good in the comparison. Now I looked at him and saw the future, looked at him and saw myself ten years down the road, drinking too much, no money, living in some rooming house somewhere, still clinging to the illusion that there actually was going to be a novel someday, having slipped from idiosyncratic to eccentric.

That was the price tag for living in society's margins, for thumbing your nose at society's conventions, a price tag that kept getting steeper the older you got. Yes, Hackett's plight had been magnified by his alcoholism, but he hadn't started out that way. He had been seduced by tennis at a young age, not only by the game itself, but the Waspy culture that surrounded it. He had used tennis for social acceptance, much the way I once had used basketball. Tennis had not only defined him, it had shaped him, too. He once had played at the Casino, the grass courts at the Tennis Hall of Fame, little more than first-round fodder in the first round of the doubles draw in a nothing tournament, had been beaten easily. No matter.

"That was the greatest moment of my life," he often said. "Walking onto that court was the culmination of every dream I ever had."

The words seemed as if they were directed right at me, haunting words. Wasn't I the same way?

Hackett always had been a victim of his fantasies. In the end he was crippled by them. He taught me the inevitable self-destruction of that way of life, even if he didn't know it. Watching him was a daily example of a life that had got off-track, and how difficult it was to get it back. No one ever gets more normal.

So I decided to get in shape, to begin to jog.

The track at Marvel Gym was up in the rafters, hovered over the court. Jogging was repetitive, boring, awful, a personal penance. The plan was to do it three days a week, and I usually had to give myself a pep talk to keep to a regular schedule. All those old things from those high-school locker rooms. Down on the court below, a bunch of guys were playing pickup basketball. I hadn't really played basketball in years. The last time I did, wheezing like some octogenarian after only a few trips up the court, I was so out of shape my teeth hurt.

"Come on down," Shein called.

"No way," I said. "I'd rather go back to basic training."

"Why don't you want to play?" Shein asked later. He once had been the captain of the Brown tennis team, still played three or four times a week, had always played. He couldn't understand how I could stop doing something that had been such a big part of my life.

"That's the point," I said. "It used to be important. It's not anymore."

I still believed that.

One day they had nine players, needed one more. Shein talked me into coming down and joining them. The players, almost all in their thirties, ran the spectrum of ability level, from a few guys who once had played college basketball to guys who had little clue. I didn't want to play, looked at guys my age who still played as foolish, trying to bring back some lost youth. By not playing, I still had some sort of superiority over those who couldn't seem able to walk away from the game. By not playing I still clung to the faint illusion that I had moved beyond basketball, however laughable that notion had become.

The times I had played in the past decade had been few and far between, and never good, always left me with the feeling that it had been some sort of sacrilege, like putting vinyl siding on an old Victorian house. Playing had been too important to stumble and bumble through a game, sucking for air, missing shots that once had been automatic.

This time was different. Maybe it was simply because it was better than jogging around the track. Maybe it was because there was a social aspect to it, not like the solitary nature of running, with each lap its own personal prison. But that first day playing was fun in ways that it hadn't been fun since I had left college. Not that it was easy. I had been away too long, there had been too many bad nights, too many times I had seen the gray light of dawn come creeping into the room. It was like playing on skates, a little unsure. Playing again was like entering some foreign country, some strange landscape where things should have been familiar but somehow weren't.

The competition, though, was instantly addictive, something that had been missing for years. More importantly, it was nice to be on a team again, if only a pickup team, a team brought together for only a few minutes at a time. Nice to be able to run and sweat and lose yourself in the act of play, your mind free of anything else, totally immersed in what you were doing, like the happiest times of childhood.

Why hadn't I played before? What had been the big deal? What kind of statement had I been trying to make? And who was I trying to make it to?

Soon I was religiously playing three days a week, all year round. Looking forward to it. Planning my day around it. And getting competitive about it. Wanting to win pick-up games. Wanting to play well. Getting upset when I didn't. As if nothing had really changed since high school, nothing at all.

"What's the big surprise?" my sister Polly asked.

"I don't consider myself that competitive a person," I said. "At least not anymore."

"Are you serious?" she said in amazement. "You'd knock me down to get a loose ball and I'm your sister. You're just like Mother. You're both amazingly competitive."

Polly was seven years younger, so we had grown up in different childhood worlds. I remember little about her as a child, so immersed was I in basketball and my own dreams. Had she actually been there all the time? But she remembered. Remembered being dragged to my high-school games as a young kid. Remembered the way those games had defined the family zeitgeist at the time.

"I grew up listening to the sound of the ball in the driveway," she said. "My growing up revolved around going to your games. I remember everything about it. The names of the players. The cheerleaders. It was all very exciting. When you're ten years old and looking for any way to stand out, having your brother as the hometown hero doesn't hurt. The guys came over to the driveway to play with you. There always was a game going in my backyard. So I became the observer."

She also had been the only one home when my parents' marriage disintegrated, caught the full brunt of it in ways my brother and I never did.

Yet we were alike in many ways, too. She wrote a column

for a local weekly paper, was a reporter, first on radio in Providence, then for a television station. We knew a lot of the same people. She also liked going to basketball games, a link to one of the parts of her childhood that had been happy. Not like my brother Geoff, who never had any interest in basketball. Once, when he was visiting from Denmark, I got him a ticket to a Celtics game I was covering.

"You've got to see Larry Bird play," I said.

"Why?"

"Because he might just be the best that ever played."

So he went, then went back to Copenhagen and told an American friend of his that he had seen that great player "Larry Fish."

"It's Bird," his friend said. "Larry Bird."

"Fish. Bird," Geoff countered. "What's the difference?"

My brother had things in perspective. Not for him the traipsing after athletes years younger than himself. Bird. Fish. Who cared? Not for him, looking back at some childhood game. He had taught himself to play the guitar, now he was learning how to make them. He had taught himself woodworking. He read voraciously, had innumerable interests, had developed an intellectual curiosity that I had lacked. He and his wife Kirsten, a Danish woman who called American culture "stupid," traveled extensively throughout Europe. From a troubled adolescence he had found a serenity, a peace with himself. Not for him to be chasing games, chasing something in his past he didn't understand.

Players come in four categories in pickup games: the ones who never played and are just out there for exercise; the ones who never played and have no clue, thus becoming dangerous to play against because they can hurt you—the old "never play against guys who wear black socks" syndrome; the ones who played and are content with that, and play now for the love of the game, with no aspirations; and the ones whose basketball reality never matched their dreams and who are still trying to prove it, either to themselves or anyone else.

There are many of these last types in every gym in the country, every pickup game there ever was. We had several of them. Each game became their Final Four, their chance to prove that somebody once screwed them over as a player.

There was Ed, who once had played at the University of Rhode Island, before he impregnated his girlfriend and got thrown off the team for breaking into a campus vending machine. He was a gifted athlete, one of the best racquetball players in Rhode Island. But his basketball career had ended too soon, and these pickup games became a personal arena for athletic redemption. He worked in the jewelry business, always was impeccably dressed, giving off the appearance of the successful businessman. Then the games would start and he was off in some private universe, yelling at teammates who didn't play well, arguing about calls, his need to win so consuming that it clouded everything else.

"I'm sorry," he said to me after one outburst. "I know I lose it, but it's like I can't help myself."

He didn't have to apologize. I understood all too well.

There were times when I lost it too, when it was all too important, when I threw the ball against a wall in disgust after a loss. We all did, for the games took on their own reality, the Final Four three times a week at noontime, every week.

There was Peter, two years ahead of me at Brown, who had flunked out and spent a year in Vietnam during which he helped get wounded soldiers out by helicopter. He had two bad knees, and often limped afterward, but played anyway. There was "Willis," who worked on a fishing boat, so named because Peter once said he played like former New York Knick great Willis Reed. There was "Shooter," who always wore a purple shirt and cheap black sneakers, circa 1955, and had long hair that cascaded around his shoulders. He was a bartender, supposedly was writing a book on a band. For the longest while, I didn't know their real names. They were just Willis and Shooter.

There was Mick, a slow, heavyset guy with a shooting touch as soft as a feather. He couldn't run. He couldn't beat anyone off the dribble. But if you didn't play him, he'd shoot your lights out. No one knew him. No one knew what he did. No one knew how he found the game. Just that one day he was there. And the next. That, and the fact that you had to play him tough.

There was a succession of assistant coaches from Brown, including one who called everyone "Doodle," and another one who once had been one of the first black players in the Ivy League, as a guard for Dartmouth in the early 1970s.

"They had to bring in all these black guys and they didn't know where to find them," said Billy Raynor, who would go on to become the head coach at Holy Cross. "So they went to inner-city high schools and asked who the leaders were. The only problem was half of them were also gang leaders. So then they had to bring us all up to school in the summer before school started and de-gangsterize everybody."

The pickup games also became a racial laboratory, courtesy of a group of neighborhood black guys who quickly found the game and became regulars.

There was "Joe Joe" who fancied himself a model, complete with portfolio that he showed to me in the locker room one day. He was light-skinned and wiry, and when sucker-punched in a fight during a game, proclaimed that he was going to come back the next time with a gun and "kill the dude that got me." There was "Big Cal," who had grown up in Shelby, North Carolina, the hometown of basketball great David Thompson. Big Cal was burly, often played while wearing a hairnet, and owned a variety store in which some of the things he sold were illegal. There was Lennie who used to run up and down the court shadow-boxing and throwing punches at imaginary opponents. He was in great shape, with the upper body of a weight lifter. He often would sidle up to someone and ask, "Do you know what time it is in Paris, France?"

There was Buddy who sat in the sauna for hours at a time, only coming out to play a couple of games before going back. There was "Sha" who traveled every time he took the ball to the basket, and if called for it, would launch into a tirade. There was Lemoyne, a quiet, sensitive poet who had done some jail time.

They were mostly from the neighborhood a few blocks from Marvel Gym. Three days a week basketball brought us together. It was the great common denominator, cutting across racial lines, cutting across everything. Guys wanted you on their team because they thought you could help them win, not because of what color they were, because to lose invariably meant that you had to sit and watch and wait for your turn to play again. In that sense we were truly egalitarian, a blueprint for a larger society.

Over several years the players came and went; the games always went on.

Complete with the chatter that went with them.

Give me the ball, he can't cover me.

You going to make one today, or what?
You better put someone on me.
Call him on the phone, let's get started.
One time some burly guy nobody knew was playing. Ed drove down the middle and got fouled hard. The next time the same thing happened. Ed jumped up, fury in his eyes. Nobody fouled him hard twice and got away easy.

"What the fuck you doing?" he growled.

"You got a token?" the burly guy asked.

"A token?" I said. "What's a token got to do with it?"

"When you're trying to take the A train to the basket you need a token."

Oh.

Sometimes the chatter took on a harder edge.

"If that was a pocketbook you would have held on to it," said Ed, as the ball went off Sha's hands out of bounds.

"Fuck you, you KKK-looking motherfucker," Sha answered back.

Nothing was sacred.

Often, a certain tension was there, part race, part class, part just plain cultural differences. Sometimes there was the sense we would never get beyond race, that it was always there, just waiting to emerge. But in our quirky way we got along. And if once in a while there were incidents and the promise of real trouble, it never truly surfaced. We learned to get along, at least most of the time. There was a bond formed, even though it often got stretched.

With few exceptions, we never dealt with each other away from this unofficial noontime league, a fact that had nothing to do with race. Guys played and went their own way, week after week, year after year. Nor did we discuss personal things, or any real details of lives that existed outside the gym. The talk was of the pickup games and the guys who played them. Or else of basketball itself, the NBA, college games. As if nothing outside the gym, outside basketball, existed.

If at first I felt self-conscious still playing basketball in my thirties, that soon stopped. I had missed being a part of a team in ways I little understood, so just being on a pickup team at noontime was a treat. The camaraderie. The sense of sharing something. The sense of having a common goal. Even if these all were ephemeral, could change every few minutes, one game's teammates quickly becoming the next's opponents, no two games were ever the same.

It was one of the special things about the game, how you could take the same bunch of people day in and day out and yet it was always different, basketball full of innumerable permutations. I had forgotten just how wonderful the simple act of playing basketball was, whether you were good or not.

And I came once again to appreciate how sports are one of the few things in life you can't fake. The ball either goes in or it doesn't. You either win or you lose. It's not like movies where there are endless takes. Not like politics where there are speech writers and spin doctors, always someone trying to manipulate the perception. There is a purity about a game, something real. And in an age of obfuscation and situational ethics, when everything seems to come in shades of gray, there is something true about that.

I also came to appreciate the game in ways I never had before. There was no pressure. Not having to score points. No cheers if you played well. No name in the paper the next day. Basketball without the baggage.

In a certain way it was better, being able to enjoy the game for what it was, not for what it could get you.

You only hit the target if you don't aim for it.

That was one of those old expressions I had taken from the sixties, one of the few that still made sense. It was applicable here. I came to appreciate the game in ways I never had before, to appreciate the actual playing the game, not just everything that was a part of it. It didn't make any difference that they were just pickup games in an empty gym. The essence was the same. Nor did it make any difference if I played well or not. I knew I was never going to be a real player again, it had been too many years. I had no more illusions. That was the good part. No expectations. No ambitions. No hopes. Just playing. Right there in the moment.

We all had various aches and pains, an ongoing assortment of maladies. It came with the territory. John the Lawyer dragged around a huge knee-brace. Peter had to ice his knees after he played. I hobbled around every morning, with sore heels, sore Achilles tendons, sore everything. It seemed a small price to pay.

So there were countless times when I would sit on the sidelines between games, the sweat running off me, totally immersed in the games, and realize how lucky I was to have begun playing again.

Even if I didn't admit it to anyone.

Christina was a doctoral student at Brown who also taught deaf students. She was Greek, with dark hair and matching eyes, and from the moment we met I was captivated. She was a curious mixture of academic and street-smart. Her father was a jockey agent in New York, a true Damon Runyon character who spent much of his life as a gambler. He was as New York as an egg cream, told innumerable stories about his life as a racetrack tout, had been featured in a column by Jimmy Breslin about going to the opening of the races with "Angelo the Handicapper."

Christina was the first person who believed in my writing, the first who said it was foolish to keep selling magazine stories for $200, the first to push me into trying to actually get the Providence *Journal* to hire me, instead of just buying my articles. Through her prodding, I finally was able to get hired as a reporter, farmed out to work in the Newport bureau to begin learning how to be a reporter.

Eventually, we married and bought a house on a quiet street a few miles outside of Providence. We even had a dog. It was the first house I had lived in in almost two decades, the first real stability I had known since my parents had separated and my mother had sold the house in Barrington. Some nights I went out on the deck and looked at the sky, the neighborhood quiet, Christina asleep, and thought how lucky I was. I was a survivor. I had survived the bars, survived poverty, survived freelancing, finally had a job that could be a career, for at some level writing was a surrogate for basketball, something to get excited about, feel a passion for. At such moments I felt as if I had traveled far from that night on the bus in February of '68 when I peered into the future and didn't have a clue.

Was there life after basketball?

Yes, there was. Fifteen years later I had found it. Or so I thought.

Still, the games defined me.

One year, on the night the season ended, I felt an incredible sense of dread. What was I going to do now? How was I going to make it until the next season?

Christina was in the kitchen. The dog was next to me. The

house was neat and clean, a well-lighted place. I finally had a
job, a pension plan, and all the trappings of a normal life. Yet
I felt an incredible sense of loss.

"What's the matter?" she said later.

"It's just the season ending," I said. "It's no big deal. I'll get
over it."

"No you won't," she said.

"What do you mean."

"When I first met you I used to wait for the season to end,"
she said. "I saw it as something with a beginning, a middle,
and an end. Now I know differently. Now I know that it's just
one big season with no end. One big season that just goes
around and around and never ends. Winter league. Summer
league. Noontime league. One big season that just goes
around and around and never ends."

That had serious ramifications for her.

She had been raised in a family of horse players, men whose
lives were regulated by the race track's schedule. Belmont in
the fall. Aquaduct in the winter. Saratoga every August. Sometimes there had been money for Christmas presents, sometimes not. The one constant had been that the men always had
lived at the track, emotionally absent. So she had grown up
with a sense of abandonment, every day another reminder
that men go off to their own worlds, secret places that have
nothing to do with women and children, exclusive male sanc-
tuaries that might as well be located on the far side of the
moon.

Now she was married to such a man.

The games became a constant friction. My way of dealing
with the issue was to say that my obsession with games was
not that bad, that it was all relative. So I would tell her stories
about others who were worse than me, people like Happy

Fine who spent one winter living in his car riding to various games around the East while he wrote freelance stories for basketball magazines. He invariably showed up at games wearing some rumpled suit that he had no doubt slept in, another momentary pit stop before going back in the car to the next game. Finally he was hired by a newspaper and had a real job.

"You can't believe how good it feels to be able to put your clothes in a drawer," he said.

I would tell Christina these stories, both because they were part of the game's subculture, and also to remind her that, *See, there's nothing wrong with me, there are some real sickos out there. I'm just minor league.*

One Saturday morning, we awoke with a clean slate, having eventually made up after a fight the night before. But it had been an ugly argument, full of the tensions that ran through the relationship like veins through a leaf.

"Let's do something really special tonight," she said. "To make up for last night."

I was silent.

There was a Providence College game that night against Syracuse, one of the big games of the home season, a game I'd been waiting for. Syracuse's star was a freshman named Dwayne "Pearl" Washington, the nickname in honor of Earl "the Pearl" Monroe, a onetime flashy star for the New York Knicks. The Pearl had been the most celebrated high-school player in the country the year before, the latest wunderkind to come out of New York City, a legend at seventeen years old, just like Earl Manigault and Jackie Jackson and all those other legends that I used to hear about as a freshman at Brown. He had a charisma that was palpable, and I couldn't wait to see him play.

"There's a game tonight," I said lamely. "You can come if you want."

"I don't want to go to a game."

More silence.

"It's a big game. Syracuse."

"I don't care what kind of a game it is," she said. "I don't care who is playing. I can't believe that after all we went through last night you wouldn't want to do something together. I just can't believe it."

I searched for something to counter with. Something to make her understand. Something so convincing it would come as some epiphany to her, so illuminating and clear that she would tell me to go ahead to the game with her blessing.

"But it's the Pearl," I said.

One night Christina came home late from a meeting, climbed the stairs to the second-floor bedroom where I was watching another game in a never-ending string of them.

"I'm tired of hearing crowd noise when I walk into my bedroom," she said. "Living with you is like living in a gymnasium."

An epitaph for a marriage.

It was the spring of 1984, my first year as a sports writer for the Providence *Journal.* I now got paid for watching games.

The perfect job.

I had been hired three years earlier as a reporter, put in a bureau in Newport covering local news, sitting in town-council meetings where politicians argued about which tractor to buy, before realizing that the worst game in the world was infinitely better than the best town-council meeting there ever was. Good-bye to the reporting life.

It had been a major decision. Not only did it mean that my days of writing about other things were probably over, it was an open declaration that sports were once again the defining thing in my life. Christina and I had talked about it endlessly on a trip to Greece in the summer of 1983, through the Placa in Athens, through bus trips into the countryside, then to the seashore, to the small fishing towns where we would sit and watch the sun set every evening, so far away from basketball. Yet throughout the trip, although I certainly didn't see it as anything revelatory at the time, I was reading David Halberstam's *The Breaks of the Game,* about a season spent with the Portland Trail Blazers of the NBA.

I started writing sports that fall. One of my beats was the Celtics, a season that went all the way to the NBA Finals. Celtics versus Lakers. Bird versus Magic. The two best basketball teams in all the world. One day I was riding through Malibu in a rental car, radio cranked up. It was a day of cerulean blue skies and a balmy breeze, the L.A. of fantasy. That night I was going to the Forum to cover the game, one of the best seats in the house, complete with a press pass.

They're paying me to do this?

The job played into my obsession, gave it a certain validity. Not only was I now paid to watch games, watching them also had become socially acceptable. Now it was not only considered normal to arrive two hours before a game, it was considered dedication. As it was to sit in the office and talk sports all day.

To Christina, though, it was one more example that I was choosing the games over her. The most obvious factor was the hours. Sports writing is all about nights and weekends. It's about dinners missed and Saturday-night games, about coming home late and tournaments that take you on the road. Too often, it's about being away, off in a generic arena where nothing ever changes except the names of the players. To her, it must have felt like her father going off to the track every day, living with a man who was not there. She had not wanted me to leave reporting for sports writing, fearful of the schedule, no doubt more fearful that the job catered to a part of me that had nothing to do with her.

The night the Celtics won the '84 title I got home at four in the morning, having to do stories for both the morning and afternoon papers. I had been to the West Coast twice in the past ten days, and to both Milwaukee and New York for playoff games before that. When I came into the house in the early-morning hours the dog barked, Christina woke up, looked at the clock and simply shook her head in resignation. The entire winter had been a disaster, her resenting my job, me feeling rejected. We would go for days without speaking, the tension building, until it would spill over in some argument that always went around and around before ending up nowhere. Or else she would be gone, back home to New York where her mother was ill, only to return more withdrawn, more remote.

So by the time the playoffs had started I was as emotionally removed from the relationship as I figured she was, immersed in the Celtics' journey through the playoffs and my role covering them. It was all familiar ground. Hadn't I done the same thing back when I was being dumped by Dinah at Worcester Academy? Hadn't basketball always been a sanctuary, a safe place to nurse my emotional hurts, some sort of salve for the wounds? Once again I went from game to game shutting everything else out, Christina included.

That afternoon she came out on the deck in the backyard. I was in a lounge chair, the long season over, looking at days off and the promise of summer.

"I can't live like this," she said.

I moved out that afternoon.

For the next eighteen months home was a small furnished apartment on Providence's East Side, two blocks from Brown. No phone. No television. No stereo system. The bed was a mattress on top of some orange crates. There was never any food in the kitchen. It was anonymous, transient, simply a place to sleep. All my energy was poured into the job, and the games that defined the job.

At one level it was the way to deal with the pain of the breakup of the marriage, the utter sense of failure I felt, the guilt. There always was another game to go to, another tournament to cover, another deadline. It kept me going through the adjustment of learning to live alone again, of trying to put some of the pieces back together. The games became my comforter, the safe harbor my shipwrecked life could find some solace in.

Gradually, it worked. Not all at once. Not without a certain amount of pain. But one deadline led to another, and then another. There was always another game to go to, a never-ending succession of them, from week to week, season to season. Eventually they took me out of myself and my own troubles. Not that that was anything new. Hadn't the game always been a place I could hide in?

Only this time it was different.

America had become more sports-crazed than it ever had been. You couldn't turn on the television without seeing some

game from somewhere. They were everywhere, a media overload. Everywhere I went people talked about games, had opin-
ions on them. As a sportswriter, there was the feeling that you
were writing about something that people cared passionately
about. I felt like I had a front-row seat at the circus.

More importantly, for the first time in many years I felt in
tune with the culture, no longer living in the margins, no
longer feeling that society was heading off in one direction and
me in another. As a kid, basketball had given me a certain acceptance. Now it was doing it again.

I had discovered that writing sports was the next-best thing
to playing them, and that realization seemed to change everything. Maybe it was as simple as that I finally recovered a
sense of self, an honest one rooted both in my past and in my
experience, not something manufactured. The demons that
had been plaguing me for years, all those ones that were becoming so self-destructive, were gone. I had found my life
again, finally.

There were nights at Providence College games in the Civic
Center across the street from the Providence *Journal,* where I
got there about two hours before the game, the building virtually empty, just a few people hovering around the court getting ready. Often, I would go up into the stands and sit there
by myself, watching the building fill up, assimilating the
arena. Invariably, at such times, I would think about how
much had changed and how lucky I was to be able to make a
living doing something that was such a part of my life, and
how I never could have envisioned that back there in that
driveway when I was a kid. At such times I felt like I had survived a long journey.

Basketball was, once again, the major component of my
life. And now it wasn't just basketball games. Red Sox games.

New England Patriots games. College football games. I moved through the seasons, taking notes, writing down impressions, analyzing, trying to look at things differently. No longer did I have pretensions of writing about more weighty issues. I was a sportswriter, paid to go to games, and it wasn't an issue of why they still were so important.

I never thought about that.

9

February 1985.

A conference at the Watergate, the infamous hotel in Washington, D.C.

I was one of about a dozen sportswriters there to deal with various issues in sports when one of the speakers said, "All athletes crash when it's over. Even the superstars. They all have a serious adjustment to make when their careers end. They all crash."

He was referring to professional athletes, but I knew exactly what he meant. Hadn't I crashed that night in February on the bus coming back from Princeton, knowing my career was going to end in a month and having no clue what lay behind it? Hadn't my entire adult life been trying to deal with the effects of that crash?

"All athletes crash when it's over."

Wasn't this the great unwritten story of sports in America?

The image was disturbing enough, for these are the people that had won the athletic lottery, the ones for whom the sports journey had worked. But what happens to everyone else? What happens to those whose careers ended long before, whether it was college, high school, whatever? The ones who never made it to the top—what happened to them? Wasn't this the great unwritten story?

So I came back from that seminar in Washington and began developing a theory, namely that everyone crashes with sports. Everyone eventually reaches a time when they confront that moment when they realize that they're just not good enough, and there's nothing they can do about it. Everyone. From the kid who gets cut from his school team, to the one-time professional superstar who has lost too many steps. It's just a question of when. And the more time you spend with a sport, the more it defines you, the more traumatic it is when it ends.

For sports are the way that masculinity is defined in this country. They are also, for many kids, the first dream. But for many kids this dream dies the first time they go to the playground and discover that they're not as good at sports as the other kids in the neighborhood. So they go home, make their separate peace with the fact that they're never going to be a great athlete and get on with their lives, sports already in the past tense.

With others, it happens in Little League, or some other organized youth league. This is the first real demarcation line, the first awareness that some kids are going to be players and some are not. Often, it's the first time adults are involved, whether it's coaching or giving approval, the first time kids are very aware that being good in sports has perks. Then it's junior high, a continuation of the same process.

For others, it's high school. This is where most athletic careers end, where the dream dies. It's a theme that runs through literature and film, the ex–high-school jock forever trying to find a second act, forever hearing the echoes of those old cheers. Like the great scene in the movie *Breaking Away*, when the character played by Dennis Quaid is watching the University of Indiana football team practice in the cavernous stadium in Bloomington. Quaid is a townie, the ex-quarterback whose career ended in high school. Unsure about the future and his place in it, growing aware that he will always be what's derisively referred to in Bloomington as a "cutter," he turns to his friends in a voice that's a mixture of bitterness and loss, and says how he used to be a pretty good high-school quarterback, but now every year he has to hear about the new hotshot quarterback at the university and "every year it's not going to be me."

But what about the ones who go on to be the hotshot quarterback at the university, the few who actually get to play in college? What happens to them when it ends, the overwhelming majority of whom never get to be pros? The ones who have spent just as much time, poured as much of their heart into it? Isn't their fall a harder one, one not cushioned by being a professional and the status and money that comes with that?

Certainly it was for me.

The game had given me acceptance, it had given me status. Most of all, it had given me a sense of self. Within the confines of the game I had a certain confidence, knew my place in the world. Outside of it, it was like starting from scratch, like working on mysteries without any clues.

I had grown up believing in all those slogans on the locker-room walls, all those values. Not only had basketball been the first dream, it had been the only dream. And when it had ended, as it surely would eventually, I had no backup, no plan, was in a free fall, even if I didn't realize it at the time.

Nor were there any ground rules.

No one ever talked about what to do when your career ended. You were simply supposed to get on with the rest of your life, like going back to school when summer was over. But what happened when you had no other life, and no real clue how to get one? No one ever suggested that this might be difficult, or that there figured to be a certain adjustment process. No one ever suggested that the death of a dream might carry a heavy price tag.

My way of dealing with it was denial, to tell myself that basketball was something I could easily leave behind. It made a certain sense in the beginning, provided me with the illusion that I could easily discard something that had so defined me. I never thought that there might be any ramifications.

For years I always had seen this as just my story, my own burden. After all, it took nearly two decades before I started to truly understand it, truly understood that being so obsessed with a sport had made me different, and the ramifications that come with that. Now I knew it was the real story of sports in America, the down-and-dirty reason why we as a society are so sports-crazed, why we treat great athletes as if they are descended from royalty, the ones who play out all our adolescent fantasies for us.

"All athletes crash when it's over."

This was the issue I had been dealing with ever since I came back from that conference at the Watergate.

But I didn't think about it all the time.

Most of the time I went to games.

But an unexpected thing happened.

The more time I spent as a sportswriter the more my obsession with games lessened. There was no defining moment. No incredible epiphany when, sitting in some gym, I suddenly realized I didn't have to be there anymore and got up and walked out, forever freed from my psychic prison. Gradually, though, there was the sense that the games weren't so vital anymore.

The first clue was at the Big East Tournament in Madison Square Garden in New York. Once, it had been the best day of the year for me, four games in one day. Now it was different. I still went. Still liked it. Still sat through as many games as I could. But there was not the same sense of urgency, the feeling that the world was going to fall off its axis if I missed a game. No sense that something terribly important was being taken from me if I missed one. Something had changed, however slightly.

No longer did I have this compelling desire to watch every game on television. More and more was the sense that if I missed this one there would most certainly be another one tomorrow. Always another game. Maybe it was something as simple as the fact that since I now covered so many of them for a living, each one lost some of its importance.

But I knew it was more complicated than that.

The games no longer were some secret vice, some compartment that existed independent of the other things going on in my life. They were right there in the open, as public as the morning newspaper. More importantly, no longer were they something I felt guilty about, or had to make explanations for. Just the opposite. Now, the more I knew about the games, the better I was at my job.

I also no longer felt the need to deny their importance. And with that acceptance came a certain peace. The obsession began to wane, slowly, steadily, like steam escaping through a manhole cover.

Not that my fascination with the games went away completely.

I still got juiced when the season started, still looked forward to the games with a certain anticipation. I still had times when I knew I was over the edge, once again chasing the game the way some cat chases his tail, around and around, oblivious to everything else. I still went to games with Cox, still analyzed them and their culture. I still went to games with Gerry Alaimo, and the ritual was always the same, even though he got fired as the Brown coach and went to work across town in the athletic department at Providence College. He drove to the game, I drove back. The only difference was that there weren't as many beers afterward.

Gradually, I began to realize that the more I played myself, the less important going to games became. Not surprising. Hadn't that been the appeal in the first place? Hadn't that been the first love, the actual playing?

"It defined us," Raffa said. "There's no getting around that."

We were coming back from watching some high-school playoff games, talking about the old glory days. "We were so good, everybody was so into it. We were the only game in town."

Raffa had stopped playing after college. His knee had atrophied, had never really been the same since his operation the summer before his senior year in high school. He now has arthritis in the knee, and in all probability is looking at a knee replacement in the future.

He coaches a Division Three college team in Rhode Island, has been coaching ever since he left college in 1968, the first nine years in a prep school in Barrington, then at small colleges in Rhode Island. It's always been part-time, teaching at the prep school his full-time job. But basketball has always been his first love.

"Basketball is everything I've done. It's everything I am," he said. "I knew I wanted to coach when I was thirteen. I loved the game so much, was so obsessed with it. And once I got married I knew I wanted to coach in Division Three because I didn't want to get on the roller coaster that's Division One."

"Was there any downside?" I asked.

He thought for a moment. He had been divorced for several years now; his wife had moved out, leaving him in the house in Barrington with his three kids. When he'd been married, his wife had come to dislike basketball, resent it. He knew what I was getting at.

"Basketball didn't ruin my marriage," he said. "I just don't believe that. If it hadn't been basketball it would have been something else. She resented basketball, felt she couldn't compete with it, but it was more than that. She wasn't happy, but I don't think she was going to be happy whatever I was doing. If I was home, I was around the house too much, driving her crazy. If I was out, I wasn't home enough. It was always something. Coaching basketball is my hobby. Some guys play golf. I coach basketball."

Shortly afterward, I went to have lunch with Sarles. Where Raffa had stayed in the game, Sarles had moved beyond it.

Our lives had gone off in separate directions, but I still felt great affection for Sarles, the sense that we once had shared something important. Of all the basketball I played, those two years of high school had been the sweetest, the two I would have taken back before all the others.

Lunch was in the dining room of the bank where he

worked, at the top of one of Providence's largest buildings, for he has risen to the virtual top of one of the largest banks in the Northeast, in charge of mergers, acquisitions, or whatever they call it in the major leagues of finance. We were the only ones in a private room that came with its own waitress. It was a beautiful clear day, and out the large windows there was a panoramic view of the Providence River, out to where it started to turn into Narragansett Bay, Barrington off in the distance.

So what did we talk about here in this epicenter of Rhode Island finance? Did we talk of deals and mergers and the inner workings of corporate America? Not on your life. We talked of Frank Eighme and Bob Schmidt, those two seniors on our team in 1962, neither of whom I had seen since the early sixties. We told a few Cronin stories. We talked of people come and gone, of playing basketball together, the things that bound us forever, regardless of the different ways our lives played out.

"What does playing sports as a kid mean to you now?" I asked. "Have any of the so-called lessons of sports helped you?"

"They are clichés," he said, "but I think they're true, also. Team sports teaches you how to work with people. Winning and losing, ups and downs, coping with adversity, all those things. These lessons don't just help you in business, they help you in life."

He was right, of course. Then again, Sarles always had kept sports in perspective, even back in high school. And by writing about sports I had come to understand the positive things about them I had forgotten in all those years I had focused on the negative aspects of my experience—came to see sports as possessing many more positive things than negative ones. I saw that all the time in the stories I did, whether it was the passion of the high-school kids in the Thanksgiving-morning football games, or the college athletes who essentially had used sports to salvage their lives, to give them a future when so many people they grew up with had none.

Eventually I came to realize that it hadn't been basketball's problem back then when I was a kid; it had been mine. Too obsessed. Getting too much identity from it. Being too seduced by it. Unable to keep the game in any perspective.

Not that I completely forgot the criticisms that had bothered me so much on the bus in February of 1968.

There is still a one-dimensional attitude about sports I find sad, as if there are sports and nothing else. In a sense it's more prevalent now than it was back in 1968, the exorbitant salaries, the commercials, the feeling that athletes have been anointed. How is any kid supposed to put sports in perspective when a culture puts them so out of perspective?

There is still an obsession with winning, from the nitwits who mug in front of the camera with their "We're number one" chants, to the college coaches who get fired for not winning enough games, to the increasing number of fans who want to win at all costs, as if nothing else matters, nothing else has any value. Too little realization that everyone can't win all the time, and that there's no stigma in not winning if you have done your best.

And the saddest thing of all is the number of kids whose entire dream is to play professional basketball, the NBA as the Holy Grail. This is evidenced by the media guides from virtually every big-time college basketball program. The overwhelming majority of the kids say "professional basketball" when asked about their future aspirations. No matter that the percentage who will make it to the NBA is statistically almost nil. Or that many of these kids aren't even decent college players. Or that for too many of them school is little more than a joke, taking courses merely to stay eligible, everything geared to basketball. This is the dream, and it's an incredibly seductive one.

These are the ones I relate to the most, the ones who are so obviously one-track. They remind me so much of myself back there in the late sixties, so many of them headed for a big fall, lemmings heading for the edge, unaware of what lies ahead.

There are still times when I wonder how different my life would have been without basketball, the road not taken. Yet that psychic battle is now over. I no longer worry about it, or dwell on the reasons why. It is simply who I am, the baggage that's always with me.

Is there life after basketball?

That was the question I had asked that night on the bus in February 1968, back in that uncertain winter when I stared out the window at a future as dark as the shadows by the side of the road. I had spent years searching for the answer. Now I knew, after a long circuitous journey, that there was life after basketball after all. Funny thing, though, it was *basketball*. Only this time it was writing about it. This time it was getting close to some of the kids I covered, as though living it all again through them. This time it was playing the game, only not the way I had played it before, not for what it gave me, but for the sheer unadulterated love of it. Yes, it's still basketball. But basketball in such a different way.

"If someone had told me when I was seventeen that I'd still be playing basketball now I would have thought they were crazy," I said to John the Lawyer one day on the way to another pickup game.

John had grown up in Bristol, one of our big rivals in high

school, two towns away from Barrington. He was a few years younger than me, had been cut from his high-school team. But he had played a lot when he was in law school, had found a game, now loved to play as much as I did.

"I know," he said. "Isn't it great?"

Yeah, it is.

One foggy afternoon in January I took a ride to Barrington. I hardly ever went there anymore, outside of going to Raffa's house which was on the edge of town, right off the highway coming in from Providence, or to the barbershop to see Nick Conti. They were my last two links to Barrington.

But on this day, for some reason, I eventually found Governor Bradford Drive, and parked on the side of the house I grew up in, right in front of the driveway.

It was just a driveway in front of a tan garage. On this afternoon, a thin coating of snow covered it. Off to the right was our house, tan now, not the dark brown it used to be. I hadn't been inside it in over twenty years. I didn't know who lived there now—didn't know anyone who still lived in the neighborhood. The houses are the same, the people are not. To the left of the driveway was a backboard with a hoop, not like the one that had been attached to the garage when I was a kid. Did that mean there was some other kid who now lived in this house? A kid who came out here alone and shot baskets in the dark? A kid with the same dreams I had?

I sat in my car across the street and saw myself as I was then, an adolescent in the driveway, shooting baskets alone, dreaming my dreams, lost in some solitary world.

It was just a driveway.

It was much smaller than I remembered. The driveway. The houses around it. The entire neighborhood. Once my world; now just memories.

I knew that in some tangible way the hours I had spent there had served me well. They got me a sliver of high-school fame. They got me into a college I never would have been able to get into without basketball. They indirectly led to making a living writing about sports, something I felt very fortunate to be able to do.

Yet I know I paid a price, too. I know that my childhood obsession defined me, narrowed my options early, shaped my view of the world. Would I have been different without basketball? No doubt. Would my life had been better? Who can say?

I continued to sit and stare at the driveway, this place that once had been so important, and thought about how capricious it all is sometimes, the way an early choice can determine so much of what happens later. We often pay for our obsessions, one way or the other. Nothing, after all, is quite what it seems, whether it's a dream, a life, or a snow-covered driveway in a quiet neighborhood on a foggy January afternoon.

But I wished I could have gone out on the court and fired up a few jumpers.

For old times' sake.

Epilogue

Even though I haven't been a real player since 1968 and now have been writing professionally for over two decades, I still consider myself a basketball player first, a writer second. Having played basketball at the level I did is still the thing I take the most pride in. Shooting a basketball is still the thing I did best in the world.

I know this is foolish.

I also know it's never going to change.

For the past several years I've been playing pickup basketball six days a week—the most since I was a senior in college.

It happened by accident. Four days a week with one group of guys. Two days a week at Brown, in essentially the same game I joined that long-ago day when I came down from running on the track. Many players have come and gone since then, but the game endures, bigger than any of us, a game that long ago took on a life of its own.

And there are many days when I'm in the middle of a game and there is no place else I would rather be, so conscious am I of how lucky I am to still be playing, to be able to get so much joy out of something that I used to do as a kid—well aware that playing basketball is the one constant, the one thing that's stayed the same while everything else has changed. I know that it's all borrowed time now, that one bad step, one more injury, and it's over, that playing will then be all about memories.

In one of the groups, we change in a small locker room that always smells of sewage. There are no lockers, just hooks on the walls. The floor is always dank. There is no air-conditioning, no windows, and sometimes in the heat of summer it's so hot the sweat starts running off you before the game even starts. Still, people show up religiously four nights a week at five in the afternoon. Lawyers, teachers, laborers, cops, one guy who once was selling cheesecakes out of the back of his truck. Basketball is the common denominator, the great equalizer, cutting through the class distinctions, making them irrelevant.

We get mad when we lose, slap palms when we win. We have good days and bad days. But we always come back.

The other day I was between games, sitting on one of the three rows of bleachers that run along one side of the small gym. My team had lost—I was awful, unable to guard my man, missing a couple of shots that used to be all but automatic. One of my Achilles tendons was hurting. It was one of those moments when I wondered why I was still playing, questioning whether it was all worth it anymore, when suddenly I had this vision of all the gyms in all the world, all full of pickup games just like this one. Innumerable games going on everywhere, everyone playing for their own reasons. Somehow it put everything in perspective.

"You're too old to keep playing basketball," the guys in the office say. "It's time to start playing golf."

"I'm too young for golf," I say, even though I know they're right. The people I began playing pickup games with are all gone now, gone to basketball graveyards every one.

Many days I am too old for the game I'm playing in, just another aging ex-player futilely trying to stop the inevitable rush of time, with just a glimpse of the glory days here and there, a faint reminder, like the words to a long-ago song you thought you'd forgotten. And there are many days when I wonder what I am doing, am convinced that it's little more than sheer folly, some hubris that keeps me playing when I so obviously shouldn't be. Basketball is all about quickness and reflexes, young legs and instinct. It is no country for old men.

But every once in a while something magical happens, time gets distorted, reality takes a time-out, and I am sixteen years old again out there in the driveway, just me and the ball, the glory days all ahead of me. My legs feel young, my body is drenched in sweat, and I'm off in a personal world that seems timeless, oblivious to everything else. And on those rare occasions, which come like gifts from some benevolent god, the only thing I care about is my jump shot.